Roden Berkeley Wriothesley Noel

Songs of the Heights and Deeps

Roden Berkeley Wriothesley Noel

Songs of the Heights and Deeps

ISBN/EAN: 9783337006990

Printed in Europe, USA, Canada, Australia, Japan

Cover: Foto ©Thomas Meinert / pixelio.de

More available books at **www.hansebooks.com**

SONGS

OF THE

HEIGHTS AND DEEPS.

BY THE
HON. RODEN NOEL,

AUTHOR OF
"A LITTLE CHILD'S MONUMENT," "THE HOUSE OF RAVENSBURG,"
"RED FLAG," "LIVINGSTONE IN AFRICA."

LONDON:
ELLIOT STOCK, 62, PATERNOSTER ROW, E.C.
1885.

CONTENTS.

	PAGE
A LAY OF CIVILIZATION; OR, LONDON	1
EARLY LOVE	34
LOVE HIDING	37
ROSE AND BUTTERFLY	39
SWING-SONG	40
MAGIC LANTERN	42
THE TEMPLE OF SORROW	44
THE GEMONIAN STAIRS	60

SEA, LAKE, AND MOUNTAIN.

THALATTA	65
BY THE SEA	76
TINTADGEL	77
SUSPIRIA	81
AUTUMN	92
MONTE ROSA	99
TO ERIC FROM THE ALPS	104
IN THE DOLOMITES	105
MELCHA	106
THE AGNOSTIC	164
THE DEATH OF LIVINGSTONE	170
BYRON'S GRAVE	177
SNOWDROPS	179

Contents.

	PAGE
NOCTURNE	180
BEETHOVEN	183
NORTHERN SPRING	187
THE TWO MAGDALENES	192
WINTER	194
IN ITALY	198

SONNETS.

POLITICAL SONNETS	201
ELY CATHEDRAL	204
VERY DEATH	205
MADNESS	206
THE SANCTUARY	207

A LAY OF CIVILIZATION: OR LONDON.

PROLOGUE.

CITY of light and shadow, height and deep,
Yawning abysm sundering rich and poor!
One upon velvet pile or marble floor
Feasts, while another starves, whom even sleep
Flieth as God-abandoned; children weep
Around their mother; at the rich man's door
She cursing God and man dies: ye who keep
High festival with morning, temple, tower,
Broad palace, rather in congenial night
Avoid ashamed the level eyes of light!
Cower hidden! royal river in your pride,
With world-wealth mantling on your stately tide,
Steal muffled in deep gloom! slow bells be tolled!
Thou on the proud dome, glistering cross of gold,
Thy life is changed to hard death bought and sold.
Art thou the hilt of a death-drinking sword
Plunged in Earth's heart by some infernal Lord?

Brethren of Him who fainted on the wood,
What help is found in yon devouring rood?
  What help? what hope? a sceptred Woman bows
Under a lowly lintel, and none knows;
Humbly she helpeth bitter loathly need,
Beareth the burden, dons the lowly weed.
Babes the high honour of their trust confer
Upon this royal lady, and by her
Perchance the city may be saved from fire,
That lurid lurks, and threats to make it one red
  funeral pyre!

UNDER awakening woods I heard the birds
With no reserve unbosom all their joy:
Even as a beam reveals the limpid deep
Of a pure pool, sweet song revealed their heart,
A shadowless illimitable bliss
Of innocent love; the joy of wakening woods
Welled over in soft frills of fairy leaves,
Glossy and tender flakelets of green light,
Infolded mutually; fair forest aisles
Dawn to leaf-laughter silent and serene;
One would surmise the new-born delicate leaves
Thronged to the ends of all the twigs to hear
Innumerable bird-song, called from sleep
By many a plumed Orpheus; their blithe notes

A Lay of Civilization.

Weave webs of music multitudinous,
Even as a leafing tracery of stems
With wayward bronze embroiders the blue air.
It seems afar one smoke above the silver
Of birchen boles ; beneath, the English flower,
The flower so dear to English hearts, nor least
When we abide among the sunnier blooms
Of alien lands, the pure and pale primrose,
Gathers in sisterhoods upon the breast
Of greening earth, her still abiding smiles,
Fair with assurance of humility.
And when their pale cool flame is far effused,
Earth in her lowlihood may vie with Heaven,
With Heaven, what time the dawning East conceives
A half-awakened light hued like the flower.

Down a green dale I heard some children roam,
Merrily laughing by a rivulet ;
Then a hawk hovered, and sweet songs were hushed
In the grove under.
All the scene grew dim,
Appeared to melt before mine eyes, and change.
I heard, and heard not, for the land dissolved,
And clouding slowly, lo ! another sound,
Akin to the sea-sound, was in mine ears,
Resembling some huge roar of a far furnace,
Whose sullen flare through wallowing mists impure

Burned like the fire-flush from those realms of Dis
In that deep-mouthed verse of the Mantuan.
Huge murmur from the throat of Babylon!
Illimitable leagues of piles confused,
Dome, tower, and steeple, stately palaces,
Islanded in a welter of dim street;
Mean habitations, warrens of dun life,
Tortuous, swarming; sullied, pale, cramped life,
With, in the midst, a large imperial River,
Turbid and troubled, the town's artery,
Spanned by tumultuous bridges; o'er them clang
Steam-dragon, chariot, horse, and laden wain,
With hurrying people of the human hive;
Whose shores are thronged with warehouse, opulent
    wharf,
Whose turbulent tide upbuoyeth bark and barge,
Throbbing, foam-trailing steamer, russet sail,
And stately ships from far sea-sundered lands.
But over all a brown Plutonian gloom
Of murk air dismal and defiled, the breath
Of our so monstrous town—her visible sin,
And weight of wan woe, blotting out sweet
    heaven!
Behold the River! a guilt-laden ghost,
How he hurries all unlingering below,
Away, away, through horror of deep night,
Pale with the guilty secret of the city!

A Lay of Civilization.

Like that sin-burdened victim, driven forth
In Israel to the wilds, ashamèd Thames
Rolls headlong, tarries nor to look, nor listen,
Hastens to hide himself in the great Deep,
There to confide, unbosom, bury there,
The tomb, the womb, the unfathomed other-world,
Absolving and absorbing Mother Ocean,
The ineffable oppression at his heart,
The horror of unutterable wrong !
How changed, O Thames ! from in thine earlier hour
Of child-like dallying among reeds and lilies,
White swans, and flowers, and boats of lingering lovers,
By Marlow, Maidenhead, or Cliveden Grove !

But darkness deepens: by the parapet
Of that great platform which embanks the tide,
While sudden lights leap to assuage the gloom,
Wavering on the water, and loud trains
Turn cloudy fiery serpents on the bridge,
I note the faded features of a girl,
Who clasps a pining infant to her breast,
And my heart, gazing into that wan face,
Named her Despair; no other name she bore
Surely among the angels, or the fiends,
Whose hate environs earth : she mounts the wall ;
Springs, and two lives have vanished in the void !

Happy birds fluting in the leafy woods,
And children playing by the rivulet !

Hard by, the glare and Babel-roar, where men
With women drink fire of forgetfulness,
Flying from ash-pale spectres of dim life
Into the burning bosom of mad fiends—
Hard by, within the gloom of the low lane,
Else empty, slouches a dun-vestured form
Of one who peers, like some gaunt beast of prey,
Yonder upon the pavement ; for he deems
He sees within the tract of lamplit stone
A morsel of soiled food, fallen casually
From Plenty satiated ; pouncing on it,
He ravenously feeds ; but one who passed
Bestows a coin within the skeleton claw
Of him, who murmurs some faint sound of joy;
And then, himself unseen, the benefactor
Saw the man kneel bare-headed on the flags,
And lift clasped hands of gratitude to God.
It is not far to where the lordly street
Hath wares luxuriant myriad-fold displayed
Behind illumined panes; the hurrying throngs
Tramp with their broken talk ; they whirl on
    wheels,
Soft-raimented, gems flashing from white shoulders,
Or swarm from forth the stately spectacle,
Embathed in yellow lustre of the lamps.
    It is a gala-night ; they laugh, they dance,
In perfumed chamber youth low whispers love ;

A Lay of Civilization.

At high doors lounge the sumptuous serving-men;
While glowing globes of emerald or ruby
Adorn, disposed with manifold design,
Each ample thoroughfare; the crimson hangs
From all high windows; launched from every steeple
Roll blazoned banners; floods of light beneath
Hail floods of sound aloft delirious,
Pealed from wild reeling bells in dome and tower;
For some imperial pageantry hath passed,
With blare of scarlet, festival and pomp
Of martial music, horse-tramp, and clanked sabre:
Our arms perchance have triumphed on far fields;
Or it may be the birthday of a king.
And yet my sombre heart reverts to him
Who snatched that offal from the pavement, sees
White retrograded faces of the crowd,
The outraged, foundered womanhood of towns;
Cold women huddling on the stately stairs,
Who cower in shadow with their babes, till one
Bids them begone; there is no room for them.

And who is here? a hunger-withered girl,
In grip of some black myrmidon of law.
Her crime, I pray you? She hath stolen a flower
From a rich lord's immeasurable land.
Her mother, poor and bedridden, so longed
To see and smell a flower: " I took it for her;

She has no friend, sir, very little food."
The girl low weeps ; the mother waits her child.
   Then was I taken through some noisome lanes,
Among ill faces bleared, unhumanized,
Like hideous apparitions from the tomb,
That hoarsely chaffered by lit market-stalls,
Into a dwelling, meanest of the mean,
Where a young child lay weeping ; crippled frame,
And hopeless face told plainly of one refused
Bodily sustenance, untended, maimed,
Scarred with habitual blows ; while cruel cold
Looks, and harsh words have laid waste her young
    life.
A man weak-visaged cowered before a woman
Inflamed with drink, and choler—father, mother,
Men named the pair—and save for reeking rags
Upon the floor, a broken chair, some shards
Of littered food, the filthy room was bare !
But pale Death looked with pity on the child. . . .
. . . . In a vault hard by of some deserted house
There lies the body of a murdered girl,
None knowing, save night-hearted murderers ;
Unowned, unwept by any man, or woman
In this confused, loud-battling multitude.
   Is there indeed no more than doth appear ?
An outraged and extinguished human soul,
Four blank dead walls, a silent senseless night—

Senseless and silent, save for our loud ears—
Around the ruin of what seemed a child?
Foul insult hath been proffered here to Man!
In all yon vain expanse of impotent worlds,
May none be found to avenge, or make amends?
Nay! if there are no Presences unseen
By mortals, unbelievable by sense,
Who have the child in charge, who bore her home,
Then from this dead-alive mad charnel-dance
Of earth let us depart, where all most wise,
Kind and heroic souls may not avail
To make our life endurable, though they,
With their poor lowly cups of cool clear water,
In this despair, and dearth, and dissonance,
Rendering fair Love palpable by loving,
Be the sole salt of our dark world's corruption!

    Happy birds fluting in the leafy woods,
And children playing by the rivulet!

    Next into neighbouring tenements I came,
Where hideous Lust with venal Force conspired
To outrage fair and feeble innocence,
By parents sold to ruin for base coin, ...
. . . . Then a voice spake: "Consider where you
    are!"
And sore amazed, I found me in a church;
But the voice said: "Lo! here they do as there!"
Here well-attired smooth dames and cavaliers

Assisted, while bland mother and smug sire
Delivered their young maiden to a lord
Of broad rich acres, and deep-dyed ill-fame,
Plague-dabbled ermine, and smirched coronet;
Her a demure priest, silver-syllabled,
Profaning holiest word and ordinance,
Offered before the altar to low gods
Of Pelf, Position, Power. The sires of old,
Jephthah and Agamemnon, immolated,
Weeping, fair daughters for the common weal,
And those pure virgins bowed the patient head,
Young victims aureoled with martyr fire;
But these, degenerate, degrade their child,
Starved on base offal-maxims of the world,
Yea, prostitute her heart to infamy,
Hunting their hollow bubbles of ill greed!
 Yonder, for guerdon of a life-long toil,
That heeds no hunger of the infinite soul,
Faint parents watch their little ones devoured
By famine; for the scanty wage,
That serves for summer shelter, fails to shield
From searching winter blasts of accident,
Old age, or illness; then the poor must beg,
Or steal, or starve, and watch their children die.

 But are not indignation, and deep ruth,
Baffled recoil, loud passionate appeal

A Lay of Civilization.

From earth's confusion to a starry sphere
Of holier Order, mirrored in the soul,
Faint and aloof, are they not very God ?
More than ill-breathing nightmares, and dull coils
Of gorged contentment, or the infinite Void,
Thronged with fair semblance ? Yea, by right divine,
These are but slaves, and those commanding kings;
They travail till the God be formed in man ;
Yea, realms of rapine, limbos, are in labour,
Till very God be born within their womb.
The Soul compels rude rebels of the night,
Passions, Ambitions, Evil aim, Denial,
To hew wood and draw water for Her need ;
All kingdoms crowned Her in the Heavens of old;
Hers are the glory, and predominant power !
O'er you lemûres, vampires, and grim ghouls,
The tranquil Queen moves, ruling turbulent tides
Of human tempest, and the outer deep
Of your wild, heaving, dark dominion.
Infernal empires, billowing in gloom,
Altho' you rise athwart the calm pale orb,
Foamingly threatening her soft sweet face,
Ye feel the mild monitions of her eye !
And Faith hath power to compass her own Vision,
Herself the fair fruit come to birth in us,
Earliest green point of the flower to be.

A Lay of Civilization.

Idlers indifferent, prosperous, full-fed,
On well-worn usage easefully reclined
In vasty mansion ; jostlers for more gold,
Or place, or power, in senate, change, and church,
Immersed in worship, sport, or spectacle,
Methought I visited ; poor homeless folk
Cowering unclothed by temple-porch and palace,
With pining babes half-hidden in their rags,
While painted harlots flaunt their own pollution,
And forms more formidable prowl ; they skulk,
Desperate, plotting cruel desperate deeds
For private greed, or violent overthrow
Of that immense, hoar, consecrated Pile,
Where the jammed People standing scarce may
  breathe,
Wide-mouthed aware of pomp of priest and king.
Then I looked stifling up to the earth-pall ;
A death-shroud, one contamination, wrapped
Round human plague, thick-woven of sin and
  sorrow !
  Yet there be wafts of heavenlier effluence
From the ten righteous Abraham desired.
For Human Love moves in the lazar-house
Of our poor planet, gentle minister.
The cloudy pall moves, lifting from the city ;
Sun gleams through rents in it on her thronged life,
On tower and temple, and the lordly river.

A Lay of Civilization.

Lo! little children playing on the green,
Or noisome alley, changed to paradise
By young enchantments of fresh fantasy;
In airy school they learn, with happy faces:
There note the humanizing spectacle,
Grave for life-lore, and for amusement gay:
While kindly Opulence with aching Need
Shares verier wealth than gold, the gentle lady,
Whom we on earth name Mercy, bends to heal
A mortal Pain, who turns to kiss Her shadow.
And hear sweet Music hovering like a dove
Over the weary! Yet are all but gleams
In lurid fume that suffocates the sun?
This huge black whirlpool of the city sucks,
And swallows, and encroaches evermore
On vernal field, pure air, and wholesome heaven—
A vast dim province, ever under cloud,
O'er whose immeasurable unloveliness
His own foul breath broods sinister, like Fate.
And yet what wealth of wisdom, and rich lore,
Swift lightnings of keen-edged encountering wit,
Fair tribute of all periods, all lands,
Wide walls alive with hues of genius!
Our pale West here meets mellow Orient,
Flowing with warm-hued raiment, redolent
Of perfume, eyed with slow luxurious fire.
All realms send sons, elect ambassadors,
For interchange of many-moulded mind.

And rarely, deep indrawn from the mad whirl
Of dissonant motion round me, face to face,
'Mid comelier architecture than our own,
I find me with the venerable shades,
Mankind consents to honour—legislator,
Iconoclast, bard, warrior, king, queen :
Richard the Lion, Alfred, the Black Prince,
That armoured conqueror of Agincourt,
And She who gained a nobler victory,
By Calais, over a revengeful heart,
True queen, true woman, Mercy's minister;
Mailed knight, with baron proud from Runnymede,
Dan Chaucer, Wyclif, Cromwell, Hampden, Charles.
There speeds boy Chatterton, elate with hope,
There droops, pale, sullen, near the agony!
Shakespeare, the human ; Milton, ocean-toned ;
Ariel Shelley ; Byron, the volcano;
Our Voice of hills and lakes; the luminous-eyed
Young Greek, astray in our dim century!

Beyond the Saxon, Norman, Roman town,
(For each whelms, founds itself on what fore-ran ;
So all lie deep entombed beneath the stones)
Where London roars, there slept the lonely wild,
Where London roars, the lonely wild will sleep.
Ourselves are founded on the lives before,
Founding the future ; will the world grow wise
With all the long-accumulating years ?

A Lay of Civilization.

A train sped on a road banked o'er the lanes,
And courts ignoble of our monstrous East;
Wherefrom glad children, laden with spring flowers,
Fluttered white kerchiefs cheering ; at a window
Of one of those poor dwellings a pale child
Waved his lean arm responsive; his hurrah
Was drowned in theirs; they saw not the wan smile
Of that seven-year-old cripple ; in a cot,
That seemed an orange-case disused, he lay,
Propped high for him to see the bright live trains
Rush past with human freight ; an ancient dame
Tended the child, his grandmother; they two
Lived ever here ; the boy knew no green fields;
Through the long days, and late into the nights,
(When her frail charge lay peacefully in sleep,
And when to wakeful voyagers by rail
The shadow of the love-invented cot
On the illumined blind appeared to be
That of a little coffin ; ah ! great Love !
Wilt thou soon lay the lad in such a cot?)
The old woman plied her scissors and her needle
For a poor pittance ; one rich offering
Of sweet burned incense, all her selfless soul
Is offered up to Heaven for the child.
The dame hath taught her helpless one to read,
Buying him Noah's ark and picture-book,

And she hath helped him order on the floor
A mimic park with turfs from a lark's cage,
Wherein are planted perpendicular
Thin sticks of deal, their foliage woolly shreds
From old frayed borders of the grandame's gown;
A baking-dish contains the mimic lake,
And, swimming there, a dinted bird, once white.
    These are unbeautiful; the neighbouring scene
Affronts our every sense; Plague, Famine lurk
With heads obscene, with sly lack-lustre eyes,
Couching at every threshold motionless.
Yet, here, yea, here, not where the lark pours joy,
Evermore pouring ecstasies in air
Of rapturous blue, nor where a throstle wafts
His incense of clear notes upon the breeze,
O'erquavered by soft shadows of young leaves;
Nor where, with age-long rapture, holy men
Dream swooning visions in Himâlayan snows—
Not there, but here I find me at Heaven's gate,
Open to let the eternal Sun shine through
On our sad Earth; fair angels come and go
In this poor hovel, for Queen Love lives here,
With dear handmaidens, Patience, Tenderness,
And her fair warrior-knight, young Fortitude.
Behold! how many graceless roofs and walls
Are glowing with a rarer, heavenlier grace
From martyr-deaths, and lowly hero-lives!

A Lay of Civilization.

A boy lay suffering in hospital,
His members crushed and mangled by a wain,
Whose wheels passed o'er him playing in the street.
Scarce can he bear the thought that he must die,
His mother's darling; she is kneeling near.
Later the father came—the man well loved
His little son, but he was harsh to her,
Paying her patient drudgery with blows.
" My lad, I cannot, will not part with thee!"
By the white bed he sobbed, to whom the child :
" Father, they tell me I must leave you both ;
I feel it very hard, but I shall die
Content, I think, if thou wilt promise me
One thing before I go "—to whom the sire
" Yes, if it lie within my power, lad!"
" Promise thou never wilt ill-use, or strike,
Or be unkind to mother when I'm gone!"
The man did promise, faltering, and then
Peace passing understanding, like still light,
Illumined the pale face of him who died.

A widow woman nursed her ingrate son
In his long illness to the final hour,
With inextinguishable tenderness,
He little heeding, snatching as a due
Love's gracious offices, a graceless churl ;
She had bestowed on him from birth till now

Through all the helpless years of his great need,
Freely her innermost, her sacred self,
And later fair solicitudes of love
Still proffered ; but, a pauper of the heart,
A boor in spirit, he had thrown from him
The pure celestial jewel of high heaven,
Which is the substance of the throne of God.
Rarely he brought his earnings home to her,
Squandering them on transitory sense ;
But her clear love welled on perennial,
Until the man died ; then the pillow soft,
Whereof she had despoiled herself for him,
Was placed by her beneath the wasted corse
Within the coffin, for she said to one
" I know well that he will not want it now
Under his thin back, yet, sir, I shall feel it ;
I could not bear to rest on it to-night,
Knowing him laid upon the cold hard wood,
And he so tired, worn to skin and bone !"
She did not long survive the man, but when
She went, her heart still turned to serving John.
And surely Love will work deliverance
In Love's own time, for time belongs to Love.

    Down-trodden woman, mother, mistress, wife,
Monotonously toiling for his weal,
Who slays you, swift or slowly, ye would shield
Him whose vile blows deform you ; now I see

In you my God, who died upon the Cross,
I hear the seraphs choiring in your heart!
Barren the bowers of Elysium;
Our very God is born from human woe!
Yea, golden fruit of the Hesperides,
A hundred-headed, tumult-breathing Beast,
A dragon-chaos guards; the Hero dares!
Fearlessly storms he the fell forest-hold,
Crags lapped in fire, or never might he find
And kiss Brünhild in her enchanted sleep,
Awakening the maid to nuptial love.
Nor was the Volsung found invulnerable
Until he bathed him in the monster's blood,
Whom erst he braved with his good brand, and slew.
Yea, Sirius, excelling our great Sun
Twofold in splendour, Sirius the fair,
How were his mighty drift imaginable,
Or lordly functions in the hierarchy
Of all Sun-gods, and their obedient worlds,
Or offices for man, without the dark
Stupendous Brother-orb invisible,
From age to age sublime companion?
    And blest are ye, dark heralds of new dawn,
Rebels, who beard the tyrant, for all souls
Claiming free-growth to their own height, with form
Predestinated from eternity.
So Pride, thrust back within the boundary,

May learn at length to recognise the Body,
Whereof we are but functioned cells, for fear
He perish isolated in the cold.
So thunders Revolution ! Hail ! unnamed,[2]
Unconsecrate Melchizedek, thou priest
Of the Most High God, though thou know Him not,
Yea, and blasphemest idols we adore,
Who have usurped in Temples His great Name ;
Without or sire, or mother, or descent,
Never enrolled among the ranks of men,
Among the living of thy land unknown,
So best to serve the people of thy love,
Young martyr, self-immured in a rank prison,
That saps the vitals, withers the rose-bloom !
There also fade thy fellows, delicate girls,
Who fondle Death with desperate white hand,
And with gay smile salute Annihilation,
Enamoured of one flame-eyed lover, Him
They serve with indefatigable joy,
Whose lofty name is Martyrdom for Man !
Howe'er insane or violent your aim,
Deniers of our Lord, I worship Him
Alive in you, Knights-errant of the Poor,
Whom His decrepit Church adores, but dead.
  And yet reserve some reverence for ranks
Of men, who guard with dedicated lives
Our holy, our inalienable Past,

Their heads bowed low before that ancient throne
Of long-descended hoar Authority!
These have mine honour also, for I know
That not one cause, but rival camps in arms
Hold Sons of Belial, and true friends of God ;
While from loud shocks of terrible crossed steel
Leaps the live flame that ministers to man. . . . .

. . . . A stately palace, whose immense demesne
Of vivid verdure is ablaze with bloom,
Whose halls are animate with radiant forms
Of picturing genius, luxuriant
With wealth of loom, and mine, art-elevate,
And sacred from the hopeless hands of toil.
The windows of the lordly pile behold
A silver water ; o'er wide miles of park
Fair antlered deer browse in the fragrant fern,
Under huge oaks, whose age-long reverie,
And leafy secrecies of summer sound
Hold more than meeteth mortal ear and eye.
But all is hushed now, save for weird, far calls
Of owls, and plashing fountain ; the lithe forms
Of statues on the terrace in the moon
Are not so beautiful as living maid
And youth, who linger under whispering leaves
And by the flowery frondage ; her light garb
Seems airy foam, a woof of silken sheen,

And delicate lace about her warm white throat.
Each leans to each with deep and dewy eyes:
The wedding-day is near; I hear low words:
"Was ever happiness like ours? the clock,
Silverly chiming from the ivied tower,
Tells how the bells will peal full soon; come death,
We shall have lived, my darling, we have lived!"
  Then all was blurred; the happy vision faded,
As if the potion of slow-poisoning Time
Were concentrated in one murderous draught,
Of power to wither suddenly; I hear
Again the troubled surge of London town.
  I pass the teeming dens where herds of men,
Shamefully heaped promiscuous, unshamed,
Are thrust by their stern gaoler, Poverty,
With scorn refused the luxury of Virtue.
  The vision taketh small account of Time,
For Time is creature of the mind that knows,
Varying with it; what was shown me now?
In a confined low garret droops a maid,
Wearily sewing with red eyes, and pale,
A withering flower, reft of air and light;
But she is very beautiful; her face
And form are moulded for young joy of love,
Tho' the rare undulation and rich lines
Be thwarted by a niggard nourishment,

A Lay of Civilization.

And the worn faded raiment be no mate
For her moon-fair imperial loveliness.
Deftly her needle plies; the long night wears;
Orion solemn passeth, and hath rest;
The weary girl may sleep not : lo! she holds
A delicate sheeny fabric as of foam,
A virginal rich raiment; surely this
Should be the very garment I beheld
Enhance the beauty of the soft betrothed
That summer evening in the calm domain,
And easeful pleasaunce of prosperity.
Whose feet are on the stair? she starts; she quivers,
Rose-colouring; the dewy, lustrous eyes
Flash luminous, the while she mutters low,
" He comes : I can no more : I wrestled long!
Why doom my prisoned youth to wither here,
Shut from all sweet fruition of my years?
How have I earned this? Honourable toil
Is ever paid here with a long dull death;
And I will live! I will be rich like her!
And wear fine jewelled clothing, aye, be loved,
Adored, enjoy my life before I die!
Ah! mother, pardon! if thou wert but here!"
A knock : one enters : he displays rare gems,
Whose lustre blinds the miserable den :
He wraps her round with passionate fierce fire;

Delicious flame consumes her; eagerly,
Headlong she plunges down the abyss of ruin.
　Sisters, and brothers, ye who name the Christ,
How may ye suffer such foul shame to be?
We would be leisured, good, accomplished, wise,
Charming, and charitable; the rank soil
That breeds the exotic is a brother's blood!
Inevitable ills arraign the Heavens:
Some wrongs accuse mankind; we challenge them.
　From where our patriot sailor on his column
Stands, with the lion of England at his feet,
Among the fountains, looking toward the towers,
The banded towers of Westminster, beyond
Green trees, by Thames, to Lambeth, London roars
Eastward, loud leagues of palaces for men
Who toil to accumulate, around the dome,
Where warrior Wellington by Nelson sleeps,
Flows to four towers, phantoms of the past,
In whose dread dungeons linger shadowy sighs
From ruined lives of all the slow sad years;
On, where the navies largesse of world-wealth
Lavish on quays vociferous (yet we
Pine ever ailing, surfeited, unfed),
By that great arsenal of war-weapons,
Forged with tremendous clangour, to God's sea.
　And westward, London roars round congregated
Palaces, where men squander. Of the crowds

A Lay of Civilization.

Our eyes encounter, some are sorrowful,
Long uncompanioned of sweet Hope, the bride,
Withering mournful; some are jubilant,
Sunny and strong with youth, or strenuous,
Of glad demeanour; listless, languid these;
But most are weary in this Babylon,
Whether men idle, or contend for bubbles;
The happiest are they who minister.
Beyond these regions, reaches of dim street,
A sullen labyrinth of ill-omened hovels:
Ah! dull, grey, grovelling populations, ye
That are rank human soil, wherein we force
Our poor pale virtues, and our venomous sins
Of gorgeous growth, our proxy-piety,
Official food, that yields no sustenance,
But chokes with outworn fantasy free life,
What hope, O people? Red convulsive strife
With those whom circumstance made masters, then
Brief moaning silence under other lords?
And yet what ask ye? Sick men from a feast
Rise loathing; health can relish his poor crust.
The pure soul hath her panoply of light,
In direst dungeon radiating heaven;
Ensphered in her own atmosphere of joy
Sees no deformity; while tyrants tread
Their marble halls, to find them torture-chambers;
A graceless prison all his fair demesne

To some illiberal, illustrious fool.
Perchance ye, ground to powder in God's mill,
May serve more than who sleep in delicate death,
With rarest incense in the mummy-fold.
    O whirling wheels! O throngs of murmuring men!
Where is the goal of infinite endeavour?
And where your haven, O ye fleeting faces?
High Westminster, like some tall ghostly father
Of olden time, stands wildered, while for crowds
Of modern men, swift eddying at his feet,
His reverend grandeur void of consolation
Broods ; for no warriors, consecrated kings,
Kings who were crowned here through the centuries,
Nor bard, nor saint, emblazoned on the pane,
Canopied under marble in the aisle,
Whose shadowy memories haunt his heart, may help.
These are unsceptred ; time trends otherwhere ;
Their slumber is by channels long deserted!
His hoary towers, with melancholy eyes,
Dream in their own world, impotent for ours ;
Or if he speak, who may interpret now?
He wakes in vain, who slept for centuries,
For he awakens in some alien world.
    Doth Hope inhabit, then, the sister-pile,
Whose stately height hath grown to overshadow
That hoary minster? This in sooth avails.

A Lay of Civilization.

And yet methinks more health is in the old,
Renewing youth from fountains of the new,
Than in rash overthrow of all men built,
With salt of insolence sown in holy places.
　Therefore, O secular, and sacred towers,
Confound your glories by the river-shore,
And marry mighty tones in ordering time!
Cathedral organ, roll insurgent sound,
As though the archangel would arouse the dead!
Our firm foundations on the invisible,
Build we the ever ampler, loftier state,
Till unaware we walk the City of God!
Yea, for I deem the fathers we revere,
Shrined in cathedral glooms, embolden us
With eyes of silent counsel, and dumb power,
Approving backs turned on their empty tomb.
But who may slay the irrevocable Past?
The Past, our venerable Sire, that girds
Bright armour round us, like some grand old knight,
With benediction sending forth fair youth
To battle, crowning what himself began!
　When England bathes in shadow, the tall tower
Of that great palace of the people shines,
Shines to the midnight like a midnight sun.
While crowned inherited incompetence,
And while law-making men laborious
Through long night-watches, in their golden
　　chamber,

A Lay of Civilization.

Wage wordy wars of faction, help the State,
The dreadful river rolls in darkness under,
Whirling our human lights to wild witch-gleam!
See yellow lamps in formidable gloom
Of both the shores, night-hearted haunts of men ;
Terrible water heaped about great piers
Of arches, gliding, gurgling, ominous !
But on the vasty parapet above
Those Titan tunnels, ghastlier for the glare
Of our electric mockery of moons,
Appears a moment a fate-hunted face—
Wan Desolation, plunging to the Void.
Then swirls a form dishonoured among gleams,
Which eddy as light-headed ; what was man,
With other offal flotsam, flounders, rolls.

   But now for one who mused upon the bridge,
Of pier and arch tremendous, the huge reek,
And sin-breathed exhalations of the city,
Transfigured by an alchemy of power,
Burned with all colour ; the broad river rose
Aslant horizonward, and heavenward,
One calm aerial glory of still dream ;
Thronged habitations on the shadowy shore
Blend solemn, disembodied to a bloom
Ethereal, bathed in evening ; fair enchased,
Or diapered upon the delicate air,

Hull, mast, sail, tiny bark, or barge, or steamer,
Poised darkly in mid primrose of the tide,
Like carven fretwork on a golden shrine.
All monstrous hostels, with interminable
Glazed bulks that over-roof the clanging train,
And all our builded chaos doth repent,
Converting into beauty; while I muse,
The mild, and modulated cadences
Of lemon fruit, shy violet, dove-down,
Deepen to very pomp and festival
Of dyes magnificent; one diapason
Of hues resplendent, crimson, gold, and green,
And purple gorgeous, like robes of kings,
Or caves of sun-illumined sea-treasure,
Or glories blazoned in Cathedral aisle,
Heart of white lily, fruit of passion-flower,
Or fervid eagle-eyes; a parable,
One nuptial-feast of marrying glow and gloom,
A wondrous parable of life through death!
 While yonder haughty heights of Westminster,
Where once fierce feuds of our illustrious dead
Sleep reconciled in monumental calm,
Mary reposing by Elizabeth,
And where with throes of living loud debate
Are brought to birth the still behests of Heaven;
With ancient consecrated privilege
Of lordly Lambeth on his stately sward;

These, and the grand dome, and the four grim towers,
Haunted by phantoms of long-wandering crime,
And harbours thronged with navies of the world,
Glow fair a moment with supernal fire.
    I am on the country-side again; but ah!
Nor here may I escape the treacherous
Flat viper-head that lurks behind all joy.
The World god-fronted hath a dragon-train,
Long loathsome coil, gold-cinctured, with a heart,
Now hot with love or hate, and now dead-cold.
Yea, under budding pear and cherry tree,
Preluding silent anthems of white bloom,
Under a nest of mellow-throated thrush,
Who warbles out his soul to a soft mate,
Her own warmth luring life from the frail egg;
Here one deemed woman drowns a trustful child,
Pleading in vain, for she is all one stone
To his close-clinging, wild, appealing woe.
Where did she drown him? Whence the bubbling
    cry?
In a pure lingering stream, that mirrors well
Fresh grass and flowers, whose home is on his bank;
He takes them to his heart, he shrines them there!
Nor ever bolt leaps shattering from the blue;
A plumy pomp of cloud in azure air
Sails undismayed; Earth shudders not for shame;
Nor yawns to engulph her—gulphs the innocent.

A Lay of Civilization.

Only a zephyr dimples with young joy
Yon vivid verdure overstarred with gold!
 Poor paralytic human Pity! what
Canst thou in this confusion? Wring thy hands,
And weep, like Rachel, for thy little ones,
Or fumble thy conjectural remedies,
That may be poisons, and experiment!
A human sire, on whom a child relies,
Asleep in perfect trust upon his heart—
Would he not give his body to be burned,
And all his soul to Satan for the child?
Death shall devour it, even in his arms,
Or Ruin rend, he lying impotent!
 But Thou, O Father, if these are thy Sons,
Canst Thou behold them prostrate in such plight
Unmoved? nor rend the heavens and come down?
Or art Thou sleeping, on a journey, or
Hast Thou deserted these thine orphans, Lord?
Nay, who but Heaven commissioneth dim Plague,
Death, Sorrow, Madness, dire ancestral Sin,
Cancer, long torments unimaginable,
And all the brood of ever-ravening ills,
That devastate mankind? No bribe can tame them,
Unguessed, innumerous, invincible.
So clings some awful beast to a faint fawn,
Galloping maddened o'er the indifferent wild.
By wells, and pleasant pasturage the Doom

Cowers in his ambush, springs from the blue air,
Falls like a thunderbolt; O men, can ye
Rival your Mother in accomplished crime?
Who perpetrates what freezes the warm blood,
Masked in light laughter, kissing while she stabs!
And yet, because the still small voice within
Reveals God more than storm, or earthquake, we,
Bettering Her rude ways, give sense the lie,
Nor will believe Her what she only seems.
O Thou dread Silence, dumbly do we bow;
In silence we commend Thy world to Thee.
   Most awful Spirit of the Universe!
Kneeling before Thy throne we grovel low,
Yea, wrestle with Thee through the long night hours,
Unknowing Thy dread Name; we will not let
Thee go until Thou loose the cloudy fold
From that veiled countenance! Hath Love, or
   Hate,
Or dead Indifference his temple there?
Now sweet, now bitter waters, night and day,
Anguish and joy, strong radiant righteousness,
With sin malformed, and folly, motley crew,
Stream from Thy bosom all impartially!
We know not; but of old a Man who bore
Upon His shoulder the world's weight of woe,
Whom men name wisest, He announced Thee
   Father,

A Lay of Civilization.

Praying, " Not My will, but Thine own be done !"
Yea, and through mystic change, or swift or slow,
Within the general bosom, and in ours,
Faith's inarticulate reason may grow clear
Fair utterable vision : the wild dance,
The strange phantasmagory of ill-dream,
Named sin and sorrow, may appear birth-pangs
Of life consummate, else impossible !

Therefore, dear birds, in leafy woods ye warble,
And you, my children, by the rivulet
Play, laughing merrily, because the world
Is sound at heart, howe'er it seems to ail.
God-fronted, dragon-trained, 'tis but a marred
Image in souls, who travail yet ungrown,
Who, ruffled, slowly waver into rest.
And why we arise or fall, no mortal knows,
Save that by change alone the unchanged abides ;
Love breathes amid the ruin of red wrong.
For a moment only of our infinite life
With one wild wing-pulse cleaving earth's rent air,
Oh ! lift we one another from this hell
Of blindly-battling ignorance to God !

EARLY LOVE.

Our early love was only dream!
   Still a dream too fair for earth,
Hallowed in a faint far gleam,
   Where the fairest flowers have birth,
Let it rest! no stain e'er trouble
Magic murmur, limpid bubble!

There two spirits in the calm
   Of moonlight memory may go,
Finding pure refreshing balm,
   When life traileth wounded, slow
Along dim ways of common dust,
As dull lives of mortals must.

Early love, fair fount of waters,
   Ever by enchantment flowing,
Where two snakes, her innocent daughters,
   Were wont to swim among the blowing,
Wilding flowers thou knowest well,
In the wood of our sweet spell!

Early Love.

Never Fear found out the place,
   Never eyes nor feet profane!
Of our innocent youth and grace
   Love was born; if born to wane,
We will keep remembrance holy
From the soil of care and folly.

No weariness of life made wise,
   No canker in the youngling bud,
No lustre failing from our eyes,
   Nor ardour paling in the blood!
Neither ever seemed less fair
To the other playing there.

Still asleep, we drift asunder,
   Who met and loved but in a dream;
Nor kissing closely, woke to wonder
   Why we are not what we seem!
Fairy bloom dies when we press
Wings young zephyr may caress.

Fare you well! more might have been!
   Nay, we know more might not be!
A moment only I may lean
   On your bosom, ere you flee,
Ere the weary sultry day
Hide my morning and my May!

Yet a fairy fountain glistens
   Under soft moon-lighted leaves,
And my wistful spirit listens
   For a voice that glows and grieves,
Breathing, when my heart would fail,
Youth from yonder fairy vale,
Where sings a nightingale.

LOVE HIDING.

LOVE was playing hide and seek,
  And we deemed that he was gone,
Tears were on my withered cheek
  For the setting of our sun;
Dark it was around, above,
But he came again, my love!

Chill and drear in wan November,
  We recall the happy spring,
While bewildered we remember
  When the woods began to sing,
  All alive with leaf and wing,
Leafless lay the silent grove;
But He came again, my love!

And our melancholy frost
  Woke to radiance in His rays,
Who wore the look of one we lost
  In the faraway dim days;
No prayer, we sighed, the dead may move,
Yet he came again, my love!

Love Hiding.

Love went to sleep, but not for ever,
    And we deemed that he was dead ;
Nay, shall aught avail to sever
    Hearts who once indeed were wed ?
Garlands for his grave we wove,
But he came again, my love !

ROSE AND BUTTERFLY.

A BUTTERFLY flew to the heart of a rose,
   Ah! more than he longed for the flower will yield!
Soft fans of Ariel close, unclose,
   Unknowing how long he may dwell in our field.

He is here! he is yonder! the rose will weep,
   'If you may not abide with us, child of air,
For ever enfolded in memory sleep,
   Here in the heart of me, oh my fair!'

Chill wind breathes, with a mist and a rain,
   Shedding the sweet petal, every one;
Now where is the heart of the flower so fain,
   And the winged blue summer elf, where is he gone?

Rose-lover, remember, though delicate wings,
   Deep-dyed in a wonderful azure of heaven,
Be turned into dust of inanimate things,
   Very soon from your own life you will be forgiven!

SWING-SONG.

    Swing! swing!
Birds in the budding wood, birds on the wing
Fill sweet soft air with carolling;
The woods no more contain their glee,
Joy brims over on every tree
In a flutter of leaves hilariously,
    Swing! swing!

Early primroses awake from sleep,
In many a dewy dale they peep;
Lo! populous land, far field and grove,
Aerial as clouds that move
In labyrinthine drifts above!
    Swing! swing!

Anemone-flakes of a veinèd snow
Lie over the sunny herbs below,
Lie over brown bents, woven and wet,
Where yellow-eyed white violet
With moss and strawberry hath met,
    Swing! swing!

Swing-Song.

Spring waves her youngling leaves for token
Dark winter's deadlier spells are broken ;
The firry roofs, with low sea-sound,
Welcome to their calm profound
The dove's long call in a love-swound,
    Swing ! swing !

Baby-boy lies on a sisterly arm
Of little maid Mary, safe from harm,
Little boy Willy will push the pair,
Hark ! how they laugh as they rush through the air !
All the young world laughs, oh, how fair !
    Swing ! swing !

MAGIC-LANTERN.

I WAS within a darkened chamber,
    Full of children small;
Upon my knees I felt him clamber,
    One of the least of all,
    Answering my call.

He was a baby of the people,
    Nor aught of him I knew;
Only the shadow of one steeple
    Abode upon us two;
    His arms around me grew.

Quaint figure, battle, bark, snow-mountain,
    The lantern-wizardry,
Arouse joy's hidden silver fountain
    To pretty wondering glee,
    Plashing full merrily.

Albeit nor now, before, nor after,
    Mine eyes beheld the boy,
When he so pealed with innocent laughter,
    Methought my own, my joy,
    Awhile with me did toy.

Athwart the drear unwarmed abysses
    Of all the later years,
He leaned awhile from angel blisses,
    To calm my foolish fears,
    To kiss away my tears.

THE TEMPLE OF SORROW.[3]

THE Minster glory lies engulphed in gloom,
With mournful music throbbing deep and low,
And all the jewelled joy within Her eyes
Slumbers suffused ; the saint, the warrior,
On tomb recumbent, kneeling panoplied,
Blend far-away mysterious presences
With a wide-seething multitude, alive
Through all the pillared grandeur of the nave,
A human sea ; the gorgeous full pomp
Of civil, militant, imperial pride,
And sacerdotal splendour, cloth of gold,
Chalice bejewelled, silks imbued with morn,
Flows in blue twilight of a perfumed air,
Flows, flashing into momentary gleam
By altar and shrine, for lustre of the lamps,
Silver and gold suspended, or mild shine
Of tall white wax around a central Night
In the mid-transept ; there the Catafalque,
The Shadow dominates, reigns paramount
O'er all the temple ; 'tis the hollow heart,

Dispensing Darkness through the frame supine
Of that colossal Cross, which is the Fane.
The huge vault under yawneth, a deep wound,
Filled full with Horror; Death abideth there:
Aye, with our lost Ideals, our lost Loves,
Baffled Aim, palsied Faith, Hope atrophied!
All the circumfluent glory-glow of Life
Mere tributary to the awful throne
Of this dread Power; all cast their crowns before It.
Yea, as blithe waters from the abysmal womb
Of caverned Earth dance buoyant into Day,
So here from fountains of primeval Night
In very deed Life seemeth effluent.

And some there be most honoured in the crowd,
From whom illustrious prince, with emperor
And noble stand obeisantly aside.
Who are they? for they wear no bravery,
Nor badge of high estate within the realm,
Whose garb uncourtly sombre shows and mean.
No confident bearing, claiming deference,
As of right full-conceded, suns itself
Proudly on these; we judge them of the herd
Of rugged toilers, whom the stroke of Fate
Despoils of floral honours and green leaves,
Fells for rough use, not leaves for leisured grace,

Or putting forth the loveliest that is theirs.
Lowly their port, whose dull and earthward eyes,
Heavy with weeping, droop beneath rude brows.
Whose light is with their heart, quenched in the abyss
That holds their best beloved, torn from them
In fierce embraces of devouring fire;
Whose souls were so inextricably involved
With these that perished, in the ghastly fall
They too were wrenched low from the living light
Of placid, self-possessed familiar day
Down to a desolate disconsolate wild,
Haunt of grim Madness, hollow Doubt, Despair:
Only the dead, more happy, seem to glide
Lower to nether caverns of cool sleep.

    Grief is their patent of nobility;
Sorrow the charter of their right to honour.
Smitten to earth, behold them cowering,
Mocked, buffeted, spurned, spat upon, effaced
Under the blood-red executioner,
Whom some name Nature, and some God, the Lord.
These do but threaten feebly with a mouth
Or hand, more feeble than a delicate beast,
Lashed for hell-torment by a learned man,
Lashed for hell-torment in the torture-trough;

The Temple of Sorrow.

The unregarded Sudras of the world,
Bleeding to slow death from an inward wound,
Deep and immedicable evermore.

To these the proud and prosperous of earth
Pay reverent homage! it is marvellous!
And yet no marvel! such fate-stricken men
Are armed, and robed imperially with awe!
Who flame sublime to momentary wrath,
Peal with mad mirth, then grovel impotent;
Who affirm not their own selves, who falter lost,
Like foam blown inland on the whirlwind's wing
From ocean, there dissolving tremulous
Where kindred foam evanished only now,
So they in the lapsed being of their dead.
They are one with these they cherished and adored,
Not separate, individual any more:
Lieges are they of Sorrow, pale crowned Queen
Over man's miserable mad universe.

What might have been fair Body grows to Soul:
From false-appearing palace halls of sense
They are delivered, into mournful worlds
Of Peradventures all unfathomable,
Forebodings infinite, wild hope, surmise,
Faith, love, sweet longing; yea, they are disturbed

From dull content with earth's inanities
By revelation of what hollow hearts,
And loathly shapes they hide ; afire with thirst,
Now will they sound the eternal deeps within
For living water, clouded and disused,
Cumbered with ruin ; their dull eyes are roused
From low rank plains to interrogate the height
Of perilous attainment or endeavour,
Where snows hold high communion with stars,
Where from aerial eyrie sails the eagle,
Calm in clear air, familiar with Heaven.
They are made free of God's eternal spirit,
Ever abounding, inexhaustible ;
Consumed, that they themselves may truly be.

Behold ! the Minster cruciform and grand,
Grows human, more than human, as I muse,
The Holy House of Life, the Crucified !
What seems the World, the Body of the Lord !
Expanded arms, and frame pulsate with blood,
Close-thronging individual lives ; His Heart,
Death, haloed with pale anguish and desire.
Even so the Sun eclipsed, a sable sphere,
Is ringed around with his corona flame,
Wherein appear weird members of red fire.
But as the Sun behind this ominous orb,
That is the spectral shadow of our moon,

The Temple of Sorrow.

Smiles evermore beneficent, so Love
Veils Him in gloom sepulchral for awhile,
That we who sound the abysses of Despair
May weave pure pearls, Her awful bosom hides,
Into a coronal for our pale brows,
And He Himself, descending to the deep,
Bearing our burden, may win lovelier grace
Of Love's own tears, which are the gems of God.

Ever the plangent ocean of low sound
Fills all with midnight, overwhelms my heart.
Lit tapers faint around the Catafalque,
And fair-wrought lamp in sanctuary and shrine.
The wan expanse seems labouring confused
With what feels like some glutinous chill mist,
Close cobweb-woof; the great Cathedral quakes,
As from sick earthquake throes; the pillars tall
Heave, like huge forest-peers, that agonize
In tides of roaring tempest: will the pile
Vanish anon to assume an alien form?
For all the pillars hurtle aloft to flame
Flamboyant, cloven, pallid, while the roof
Reels riven; yet there is not any sound.
Lo! every Christ on every crucifix
Glares with the swordblade glare of Antichrist!
While on the immense-hewn flanking masonry,
Scrawled, as by finger supernatural,

The Temple of Sorrow.

As in Belshazzar's banquet-hall of old,
Behold the "*Mene ! mene !*" but the realm
Divided is the royal realm, the soul !
The guilty soul, ingorged by the dim fiend
Of loathsome, limbless bulk, Insanity !
In dusk recesses how the shadows wax
Palpable, till they palpitate obscene,
Clinging, half-severed ; our sick souls are ware
Of some live Leprosy, that heaves and breathes
Audibly in the impenetrable gloom.

Hear ye the moans of muffled agony
By yonder altars of the infernal aisle ?
Marmoreal pavements slippery with blood !
While all the ghastly-lit ensanguined space
Quickening teems with foul abnormal births ;
Corpse faces scowling, wound about with shrouds,
Sniffing thick orgy fumes of cruelty,
Steal out, or slink behind in the shamed air.
Vast arteries of the dilating pile
Pulsate with ever denser atom-lives
Unhappy ; do mine eyes indeed behold
Those holy innocents, whom she of yore,
The Voice in Ramah, wept so bitterly,
Rachel, sweet spirit-mother of their race ?
They are holy innocents of many a clime,
And many a time, some murdered yesterday,

And some still languishing in present pain :
Dumb women, with marred faces eloquent,
Hold their wan hands ; while all around, beneath
Among their feet, what seems a harried crowd
Of gentle beings, who are man's meek friends.
They in the reeking shadow yonder fawn
Upon dyed knees of things in human shape,
All hell's heat smouldering in lurid eyes,
And Cain's ensanguined brand upon their brow,
Who on Christ-altars, prostitute to sin,
Offer these innocents to fiends whose names,
Obsequious to the inconstant moods of man,
Vary elusive, and deluding ; now
They are called Moloch, Baal, Ashtaroth,
Hatred, Revenge, War, Lust, Greed, Might-is-Right,
Now Church, the Truth, the Virgin, or the Christ,
But in a later time Expediency,
Weal of Man, Nature, Lust of Curious Lore.
The accurst oblation of fair alien lives,
None of their own, they pour to satiate
The hydra-headed, demon brood obscene.
These are devoured with ever subtler pangs
Cunningly heightened, fuelled, nursed, prolonged
By cold, harsh hearts, one adamant to woe,
Or cruel, infamous appetite for pain.
Ay, and of horrors loathlier than these
The verse dares name not, thrust on beautiful

Maidens and babes defenceless, of such feasts
The God-deserted souls are gluttonous—
All Nature pales at Satan's carnival!

   Who are the lost souls? Legion is their name.
Noble, pope, cardinal, king, refuse vile
Of crime-infested cities. I behold
Borgia, Caligula, Napoleon,
Marat, De Retz, and he that did to death
The royal child, who heard the angels call
Him home, soft singing, dying, ere he died.
And some are here who cumber earth to-day
Flesh-girt ; their name shall not profane the page.
There go seducers, they who lightly break
Warm simple hearts who trust them: there are some
Who wither women slowly with harsh looks,
Ill words, or blows, inflamed, obsessed by fiends,
Wearing the semblance of a flask of fire.
Yonder fair dames white-bodied, and dark-souled !
Mothers we find, who can withhold unshamed
The high and holy dues, that all beside
Of animated nature punctually,
With rapturous devotion, consecrates,
The dear debt to the fruit of our own womb,
What strength owes to dependent feebleness,
Reason full-orbed to shyly-opening sense,

Confided and confiding : even now
Their mothers gave themselves for these, and God
Bestows Himself on every living thing
For ever : these will starve, or drown their babes,
Enthral them to a ghastlier than death,
That he may work on them his loathly will,
Corrupting soul and body. Drop the veil !
All here, foul traitors ! all betrayed the trust
Nature imposed, while only dyed less deep,
Who, passing, drawled, "Am I my brother's
    keeper ?"

White victims, immolated for the world !
Ye tyrants, ye alone are miserable !
For whom Hate hath left loving, though a beast,
Is nearer God than you, removed from Him
By all the hierarchies of all worlds !
But these have fallen to abysms of pain,
And you to sloughs of inmost infamy,
That all the spheres may learn for evermore
The treachery of sweet ways that are not Love.
Yet if some God be lingering in you,
Your own eternal selves consenting not,
(Which are by lapse, and by recovery)
Touching the lowest deep ye shall recoil !
When in the furnace heated sevenfold
More than the wont, fierce furnace of God's wrath,

Blasted, ye shrivel, your inhuman pride
Stern, stubborn metal swooning to weak air
In the white heat of Love's intolerable,
Ah! then will not the innocence ye wronged,
Leaving her own bliss for you, fly from heaven
To heal you by forgiveness? May it be!

Yea, there are fleeting gleams from the All-fair,
Playing of children, larks, and lovers gay,
Beautiful image, grand heroic deed,
Cheery content; but ah! the grim World-woe
Absorbs all vision, overwhelms the heart!
A few, with seraph pity in clear eyes,
And flashing swords retributive unsheathed,
Sore-pressed and wounded, wrestle with the foe,
Defeated, slain, delivering; while aloft
We seize anon some glimpses of august,
Benignant countenances, with white wings,
As of Heaven's host invisible drawn up
For battle; but I know not who prevail.
A few pale stars in chasms of wild storm!
Aliens, alas! no potentates of ours.
We are in the power of Darkness and Dismay,
Anguishing God-forsaken on the cross!
Yea, sons of Belial with jaunty jeer
Ask where thou hidest, Lord! the Avenger! God!
Devils a priestly scare to them, who know not

Devils allure them blind into the pit.
Could they but hear low ghastly mirth convulse
Shadowy flanks of these live Plagues in air!

Mine eyeballs seared with horror, and my heart
One writhing flame, I prayed that I might die,
And lay me down to sleep with *him* for ever!
A sevenfold darkness weighs upon my soul:
I hear no groans, no music; all is still,
Even as the grave: one whispers of the Dawn:
Once I surmised the morning gray, not now:
Nor in the chancel, whose wide wakeful orb,
Solemnly waiting, ever fronts the East,
Nor in the cold clerestories of the nave.
One whispers of the lark; I hear no bird.
And yet I know the seraph eyes of Dawn
Find in her last, lone hollow the veiled Night.

Hearken! a long, low toll appals the gloom!
Like a slow welling blood from a death-wound
In the world's heart, that never will be staunched,
Crimsoning the void with waste expense of pain!
Another, and another, vibrating!
A phantom bell tolls in the abysmal dark
The funeral of all living things that be.
I, turning toward the Catafalque, desire,
Plunging within the gulf, to be no more. . . .

When, lo! some touch as of a healing hand.
For while I knew the mourners only saw
Flowers on fair corses and closed coffin-lid,
I grew aware of souls regenerate
Afar, sweet spirits raimented in white,
Who leaned above the Terror with calm eyes;
And for a moment their purged vision cleared
Earth-humours from mine own, till I beheld
No deadly Dark—a lake of living Light,
A mystic sphere, the Apocalyptic main!
Heaving with happiness that breathes, a home
For all dear spirits of the faded flowers
Outrageous men have pulled and thrown away;
Clouds in blue air reflected in a mere,
Or roseflush in rose-opal, a shy dawn
In lakes at morning, so the souls appeared.

My little children, do I find you here?
All here! Among you smiles our very own.
Each little one hath, nestled in his bosom,
A delicate bird, or elfin animal.
White-clustered lilies, beautiful as morn,
In wayward luxury of love's own light
Eddying, abandoned to love-liberty!
Joy-pulses of young hearts unsulliable
Weave warbling music, a low lullaby.
I fancy they have syllabled a song:

The Temple of Sorrow.

We are fain, are fain,
Of mortal pain,
We are fain of heavenly sorrow,
As a gentle rain,
She will sustain,
Wait only till to-morrow !

Among death-pearls
Of dewy curls,
O little ones in anguish !
The Lord hath kissed,
I would ye wist
For all the world ye languish !

The loveless world
Lies love-impearled
From innocency weeping ;
Wan wings be furled,
And you lie curled
In Love's warm haven sleeping.

For when ye know
What glories flow
For all from childly sorrow,
A flower will blow
From your wan woe
Within the wounded furrow.

We are fain, are fain
Of mortal pain,
We are fain of heavenly sorrow;
As a gentle rain
She will sustain,
Wait only till to-morrow!

So pure, pellucid fays enjoy the calm
Of summer seas, and woven waterlights
In faëry cavern, where the emerald heart
Lies heaving, or blue sheen on a warm wave.
And ye are fair-surrounded with lost Love,
Celestial Vision, vanished Hope, Desire,
Lovelier recovered, gloriously fulfilled
With a Divine fulfilment, more than ours.

There, in the midst, the likeness of a Lamb,
That had been slain, whose passion heals our hurt,
Wearing a thorn crown, breathing into bloom!
Lo! if ye listen intently by the light,
Ye hear a winnowing of angel wings,
Nearing, or waning: while from far away,
I'the Heart of all, what revelation falls? . . . .
A sound, oh marvel! like a sound of tears!

Pain ever deepens with the deepening life,
Though fair Love modulate the whole to joy.

A myriad darkling points of dolorous gloom
Startle to live light; subtle infinite veins
Of world-wide Anguish glow, a noonlit leaf.

All vanish : there is dawn within the fane;
Born slowly from the wan reluctant gloom
Conquering emerges a grand Cross of Gold,
And all the nations range around serene.

THE GEMONIAN STAIRS.[4]

ONLY a slave in Rome of old,
    A slave for whom none cares!
Slaughtered in dungeon-deeps, and rolled
    Down the Gemonian stairs;
Insulted, marred, exposed to view,
    With other human lumber,
There in the Forum, where the Roman concourse grew
    Around his mortal slumber.
There in the Forum, by the mighty walls,
    And columns hero-crowned,
Whose mourning voice upon the slumberer calls?
    The whine of a poor hound!
He will not leave the swarthy clay,
    He licks the rigid face;
Harsh-laughing, stern men in long-robed array
    Gather about the place:
One pitying hath offered bread;
    The dog but lays it down

The Gemonian Stairs.   61

Before the dumb mouth of the master dead ;
    Whose body later thrown
In turbid Tiber's flood he follows,
    Borne headlong by the river,
To lift it from the strong, loud gulf that swallows,
    Struggling, till both have sunk for ever.

A gleam is for a moment cast
    Over oblivion :
The dead slave, whose dog holds him fast,
    Drifts, passes,—all are gone. . . . .

. . . . Behold ! yon broken-hearted hare,
    With hounds and hunters after her !
And sweet, shy poet-birds of air,
    Startling from man the murderer !
And seals we flay for their sleek fur !

Ah ! what a wail of agony is torn
    From all these innocent martyr-races,
Writhing beneath man's cruel scorn,
    Whose tyrannous hell distorts their faces !
A cloud of shame clothes earth forlorn,
    Shrouds her among the starry spaces.

SEA, LAKE, AND MOUNTAIN.

THALATTA.

WHEN Love is fading from thy path, a faint remembered gleam,
Whose wond'rous glory crowned thy crest in youth's triumphal morn,
When Friendship yields a willow-wand, once in Love's generous dream,
Leaned on with all thy weight of soul, defying doubt and scorn,
Once deemed inviolable, divine, an oaken staff, a stay,
Never to fail thee at thy need in all the perilous way;
When thou art tossed from surge to surge, a helpless waif of ocean,
While hell-born lusts and base-born gusts befool thee with vain motion;
When foolish wants and angers in ignoble eddies whirl
A human spirit, formed to front God's glory unashamed;

Nor any Cause colossal, like a catapult, may hurl
To splendid goals all powerful souls, chafing, unloved, unnamed :
Then, poet, seek alone resounding hollows of the sea,
And plunge thy sullen soul in ocean's grand immensity !
  Dare to scale the water mountains ! let
  them topple in loud ruin
O'er thee, lusty swimming from cliff-harboured sandy coves ;
Though stress of tides impetuous threaten thine undoing,
Or violent swirl of undertow, where seething emerald moves
Around rude reefs and promontories, menace with swift death,
Confront the glorious wild Power, who plays with human breath !
Yea, let thy reckless shallop dare seas rushing round the caves,
Smite with straining oar the kindling heavy night of waves !
Climb the sea-crag, hand and foot, little careful of a fall !
Storm shall be thy requiem, fairy foam thy pall.
Ah ! mighty boisterous blown breath, your siren song for me !

Thalatta. 67

I quaff exhilarating draughts of wine from forth
  the sea,
Soft seething masses of fair froth luring deliciously!
Vaporous blast! voice of vast long sibilant sea-
  thunder!
Bellowing explosions in abysmal cavern-halls!
Storm my sense with sound imperial, with a joy
  sublime and wonder!
Throned aloft in perilous places unto me the
  Mother calls.
Hear Her! tremble not! but echo to the glowing
  spirit's core;
It is Her voice; Her sons rejoice; they shout to
  Her again:
By sacred river-fountains, in the desert blast, and
  roar
Of bounding cataracts, in forest, by foam-moun-
  tains of the main,
In the grand Atlantic chaos, in his elemental war,
She converses; I have heard Her; I would hearken
  evermore!
Ye, my brothers, loved and worshipped; all your
  music rolls with hers!
Human sounds inform the wind that like a trumpet
  stirs!
. . . . Verily I deem I hear above the tumult of
  the blast,

That takes my breath, and dashes all the salt spray
  over me,
Not the sea-mew's cry, nor wind's wail,
        . . . . . eerie tones of some who
  passed,
Wailing in the wind's wail, shadows drifting desolately!
For they say the drowned must wander on the
  cliffs or on the wave,
Where the fatal moment plunged them in their
  " wandering grave."
      Travelling mountain range, following mountain range!
Now the foremost wavering green crest begins to
  smoke;
Breaks at one place, and suffers dark precipitous
  change,
Arching slowly, solemnly; under where it broke
A heavy shadow haunteth the grim wall; till
  emerald,
All the cliff falls over, tumbles a dead weight
Of crushed and crashing water
          . . . . yonder unenthralled,
A monstrous buffalo in headlong strong tumultuous hate,
Plunging wild hatred upon the rock! immense
  white tongues of fire

Thalatta.

Are hurled around, enshroud, envelope with a cloud;
Lo! where springs to Heaven a fairy fretted spire!
Or is it a wan warrior's arms thrown up in death's despair?
Death-white, baffled in grey air! . . . .
Shattered upon his iron Doom in armoured onset there!
Niagaras upthundering, foamy avalanches,
Beetling, flickering huge crags of seething snowy spume,
Wherein are caverns of green tint among pale coral branches,
And white comets thwart more shadowy froth-precipice's gloom!
Dark founded isles evanish in the flying mountain tomb;
Albeit their wave-sculptured forms defiantly abide
Under grey vapours hurrying o'er the sombre tide:
Torn from parent shores, around their pillowed isolation
Ocean revelling roars with terrible elation!
 Afar, in the dull offing of a furrowed sullen sea,
O'er yon rock-rooted Pharos rises awfully,
Like a Phantom, rises slowly a white cloud,

Scales the lofty lanthorn where three human hearts
    are bowed,
Bowed awhile, involved within the Sea-Plume that
    ascends,
Swallowing a hundred feet of granite ere it bends.
        Behold! the sweep of mighty crags, whose
        league-long fortress front,
Whose frowning granite arc defies with stature tall
    and steep
Ocean's embattled billows: these have borne the
    brunt
Of terrible assaults! the cannon thunders, and a leap
Of smoke ascends the ramparts of a breached and
    broken keep,
At each discharge :
             The Titan targe hath pinnacle
    and tower :
Or is the whole an organ for the surge to smite
    with power,
That hath the turbulent storm-music for everlasting
    dower ?
        Cathedral Heights of Titans, hewn by
        colossal Hands,
Millennial ministers of flood and frost, wild earth-
    quake and fierce fire !
Lo ! where a porphyry portal of the mountain
    heart expands,

Thalatta.

Portentous shadowy buttress, weather-goldened
  spire;
There multitudinous waters wander greyly in the
  gloom;
Within the high sea-sanctuary a god dispenses
  doom;
In and out they wander, sombre courtiers by the
  gate,
Where a dim Sea-Presence broodeth in solemn
  sullen state—
Where no mortal breath dare whisper, only hollow
  sounding surges,
A welter of wild waters with their melancholy
  dirges.
  Behold they rave in echoing cave their
    wrath rent long ago,
Rent for a lair, where grim Despair rolls shoulder-
  ing to and fro;
To and fro they furious roll prodigious boulders,
Rounding them like pebbles with huge Atlantean
  shoulders.
  Beyond one vast rock-sentinel guarding the
    awful court,
Surrounded and o'ershadowed by walls perpendi-
  cular,
Before those palace-portals foamy serpents huge
  resort,

Wallowing upon the wilderness, grey and cold afar;
While among the tumbled boulders, before the
  giant cave,
Robed in royal purple, royal raiment of the wave,
Lie crunched and shattered timbers, ribs of mighty
  ships;
Yea, and limbs of some who, craving one more kiss
  of loving lips,
Were stifled in the violent froth, jammed beneath
  black stones,
Whose glossy weed may dally with their coral-
  crusted bones.
  Tall, gaunt Phantom yonder, warding portals
  of the night,
With silent, sweeping stature growing from the
  eastern wall,
Lank long arms upraised, and curving with the
  vasty cavern's height,
A beaked monster face between them, looking
  downward to appal!
Art thou stone, or art thou spirit, fearful Shadow
  weird and grey,
Daring mortals to advance beyond their precincts
  of the day?
  All the cliffs are shrouded to the waist, or
  only loom
Head and shoulders through a death-mist, but
  where the rollers boom

Thalatta. 73

Their feet are bare and stern : pale sand I discern
Near their ruined grandeur ; a chrysoprase pale
    green
Narrow water isles it, with a restless flow ;
The tidal heave advances; cormorants of swarthy
    mien
Squat on rocks about the cave, or dive in deeps
    below.

    While sweet samphire, with tufted thrift,
        glows in clefts above,
Ever and anon a sound, with ominous power to
    move,
Wanders from the wilderness, a very mournful
    spell :
Through the wind and wave embroilment ever tolls
    a passing bell.
Whence the warning ? what imports it ? When I
    clamber, when I rest,
It seems to breathe foreboding in a fading air.
Is it from the sombre church in lonely glen de-
    prest?
There, by old cross and coffin-stone, on immemorial
    chair
Of rude grey granite, hoary ghosts in dark conclave
    may brood :
Nay ! but the tolling tolleth from the turbulent flood

Not from where the giants hewed them vasty seats
   of solid rock,
Or Druid with poured human blood adored the
   Logan block :
Not from where the Cromlech ponderous, and
   hoary cirque remain,
Though we know no more who reared them, Celt
   or Dane, or Athelstane ;
Nor whose the mouldered dust in yonder urns of
   perished prime,
Bard's, or warrior's, who flared a moment in the
   hollow Night of Time !
—There on dreary moorland haunteth owl and
   raven ;
There at moonrise hoots the rocky carn, to con-
   found the craven,
While fiends are hunting dark lost souls who are
   shut out from Heaven—
The knell is knolled by wild white arms of surges
   ramping round
The fatal reef, where mariners are drifted to be
   drowned !
It is the Rundlestone!   He knolls for passing
   human souls :
It is the voice of Doom from forth profound
   Eternity !
   Weird dragon forms, roughened in storms, a
      foamy beryl rolls

Thalatta.

Ever around you, dumb and blind stones, who confront the sky !
I feel that in your soul there slumbers a dim Deity.
. . . . Were it not better to dissolve this chaos of the mind,
And in the twilight of your world long consolation find,
Restoring the proud Spirit to your elemental Powers,
Dying into cliff, and cloud, and snowdrift of sea flowers?
. . . . Vanishes the storm-rack in the gleaming West :
A long wide chasm, glowing like a World of Rest,
O'er the dusk horizon opens, whereinto
Visionary domes arise, and towers of tender hue!
A holy realm of Silence, a city of deep Peace,
Where Death leads all poor prisoners who have won release!
Long ranks of high surges, heaving dark against the bright
Heaven, fall illumed 'thwart iron crags, whose frown relents to Light.

Land's End, 1875.

BY THE SEA.

Ah! wherefore do I haunt the shadowy tomb,
My joyless days and nights among the dead?
Know you not He, my radiant Sun, who fled
With hope uncertain soothes yon awful gloom
Afar, upon the weltering sea's wan lead?
Behold! faint, tremulous, ghostly gleam illume
The unrevealing mystery of Doom,
Ashpale dumb wastes, impenetrable, dread,
O'erwhelming purple incumbent o'er the coast.
Into the Presence-Chamber of dim Death
He hath been summoned! and I hold my post
Here on the threshold, thirsty for one breath
Released from yonder! Leave me! I love my night,
More than abounding pulses of your light!

TINTADGEL.

TINTADGEL, from thy precipice of rock
Thou frownest back the vast Atlantic shock!
Yet purple twilight in cathedral caves,
Moulded to the similitude of waves
Tempestuous by awful hands of storm,
Along whose height the formidable form
Of some tall phantom stands on guard ; huge boulders
From iron crags reft, toys of ocean shoulders,
And thine own venerable keep that yields
To slow persuasion ancient Nature wields,
Inevitably sure, forbode thy fall :
For she compels the individual
To merge in the full manifold of Her
His cherished privacy of character :
And therefore Arthur's ancient ramparts range
From human fellowship to nature, change
To semblance of the fretted weathered stone,
Upreared by mystic elements alone.

That old grey church upon the sheer black crag,
Where generations under the worn flag,
Or in God's acre sleep! There one dark morn
I worshipped—heights of heaven all forlorn
With drift confused, wild wind, and the blown rain—
I mused of those who in the lonely fane
Halted world-weary through the centuries;
Kelt, Saxon, Norman, English; on their eyes
The dust of Death; Oblivion holds the psalms,
Where now in turn we celebrate the calms,
The Sabbath calms with hymns, and chanted prayer.
But what indignant wail of wild despair
Storms at the doors and windows, shakes the walls?
Before the void unsouled sound that appals,
Our human hymns in that dim sheltered place
Seem to fall low, to cower, and hide the face.
Awhile faint praise wins victory; uproars
On overshadowing vans without the doors
Whirlwind insurgent, as in awful scorn,
To be controlled no longer, nor forborne,
Of poor brief fluttering human hopes and breath,
Played with a moment by the winds of death,
Ere dissolution and dismemberment
In the undivine, dim void where all lie shent;
A shivering foam-flake, or a timid light
Spat upon by the rains, extinguished quite!
We laughin fair pavilions of light Love,
Or worship in the solemn, sacred Grove,

Tintadgel.

We rest in warm Affection built to last :
And all will leave us naked to the blast !

What means the wind ? Yon ruin's proud decay—
We know not who in far off years did lay
The strong foundations : Arthur, Guinevere,
And Lancelot, were they indeed once here ?
Are all fair shadows of a poet's dream,
Or did they ride in the early morning beam,
Armed, and resplendent, radiant within,
Champion redressors, quelling tyrant Sin,
Slaying grim dragon Wrongs, who held in ward
The maiden Innocence ; from Joyous-Guard,
Camelot, or Tintadgel, brave and glad,
Did they indeed ride, Lancelot, Galahad ?
Have lawless love, and Modred swept to ground
That glorious order of the Table Round ?
Who knows ? they are but creatures of the brain ;
Or if they were, behold our mightiest wane,
With all their sounding praise, like dream-shadows,
Storm-rack that drifts, or billowy foam ! none knows
Whether they were, or were not ; sombre keep,
And chapel crown twin crags, one ruin-heap,
While the sea thunders under, and between,
And cliffs no hand hewed mimic what hath been

In weathered buttress, pinnacle, and tower!
Where now the prancing steed, the lady's bower?
No clang of arms, no battle bugle blown,
Only in sounding cave the wild sea clarion!

But then my heart responded to the blast,
I deem that in those clouds of the dim past
Tall god-like forms loom verily; with us
Dwell souls who are not less magnanimous.
They pass, yet only to be self-fulfilled;
They pass, yet only as the All hath willed,
To enter on their full-earned heritage,
More righteous, and momentous wars to wage;
And if those heroes were not, then the mind
That holds high visions of our human kind
Is mightier than mighty winds and waves,
And lovelier than emerald floors of caves.
Nature Herself is the high utterance
Of holy gods; we, half awake in trance,
Hear it confused; through some half-open door
We hear an awful murmur, and no more:
We are under some enchantment; lift the spell,
What mortal then the wondrous tale may tell?

Tintadgel, 1884.

SUSPIRIA.[5]

Lines addressed to H. F. B.

Do you remember the billowy roar of tumultuous ocean,
   Darkling, emerald, eager under vaults of the cave,
Shattered to simmer of foam on a boulder of delicate lilac,
   Disenchantless youth of the clear, immortal wave?
Labyrinths begemmed with fairy lives of the water,
   Sea-sounding palace halls far statelier than a King's,
Seethe of illumined floor with a never-wearying motion,
   Oozy enchased live walls, where a seamusic rings?

   Do you remember the battle our brown-winged arrowy vessel
Waged with wind and tide, a foaming billowy night,
To a sound as of minute guns, when gloomy hearts of the hollows
   With sullen pride rebuffed invading Ocean's might?

Do you remember the Altarlet towers that front the cathedral,
    Dark and scarred sheer crag, flashed o'er by the wild sea-mews?
How they wheel aloft lamenting, souls of the ululant tempest!
    And the lightning billows clash in the welter Odin brews!

    A sinister livid glare from under brows of the Storm-Sun!
Brows of piled-up cloud, threatening grim Brechou,
Bleaching to ghastly pale the turbulent trouble of water,
    While the ineffable burden of grey world o'er me grew!
Yea, all the weary waste of cloud confused with the ocean
    Fell full-charged with Doom on a foundering human heart:
Our souls were moved asunder, away to an infinite distance,
    While all the love that warmed me waned, and will depart.
Fiends of the whirlwind howl for a wild carousal of slaughter

Suspiria.

Of all that is holy and fair, so shrills the demon
    wail ;
Ruin of love and youth, with all we have deemed
    immortal !
My child lies dead in the dark, and I begin to
    fail !
Wonderful visions wane, tall towers of phantasy
    tumble ;
    I shrink from the frown without me, there is no
        smile within ;
I cower by the fireless hearth of an uninhabited
    chamber,
    Alone with Desolation, and the dumb ghost of
        my sin.

        I have conversed with the aged ; once
            their souls were a furnace ;
Now they are gleams in mouldered vaults of the
    memory :
All the long sound of the Human wanes to wails of
    a shipwreck,
    Drowned in the terrible roar of violent sons of
        the sea !
    In the immense storm-chaunt of winds and waves
        of the sea !
And if we have won some way in our weary toil to
    the summit,

Do we not slidder ever back to the mouth of
  the pit?
When I behold the random doom that engulphs
  the creature,
I wonder, is the irony of God perchance in it?
'Tis a hideous spectacle to shake the sides of fiends
  with laughter,
  Where in the amphitheatre of our red world
    they sit!
Yea, and the rosiest Love in a songful heart of a
  lover,
  Child of Affinity, Joy, Occasion, beautiful May,
May sour to a wrinkled Hate, may wear and wane
  to Indifference,
  Ah! Love an' thou be mortal, all will soon go
    grey!
O when our all on earth is wrecked on reefs of
  disaster,
  May the loud Night that whelms be found
    indeed God's Day!

  Our aims but half our own, we are drifted
    hither and thither;
  The quarry so fiercely hunted rests unheeded
    now;
And if we seized our bauble, it is fallen to ashes,
  But a fresh illusion haunts the ever-aching brow.

Suspiria.

Is the world a welter of dream, with ne'er an end,
    nor an issue,
Or doth One weave Dark Night, with Morning's
    golden strand,
To a Harmony with sure hand?
Ah! for a vision of God! for a mighty grasp of
    the real,
Feet firm based on granite in place of crumbling
    sand!
O to be face to face, and heart to heart with our
    dearest,
Lost in mortal mists of the unrevealing land!
Oh! were we disenthralled from casual moods of
    the outward,
Slaves to the smile or frown of tyrant, mutable
    Time!
Might we abide unmoved in central deeps of the
    Spirit,
Where the mystic jewel Calm glows evermore
    sublime!
The dizzying shows of the world, that fall and
    tumble to chaos,
Dwell irradiate there in everlasting prime.
But the innermost spirit of man, who is one with
    the Universal,
Yearns to exhaust, to prove, the Immense of
    Experience,

Explores, recedes, makes way, distils a food from
 a poison,
 From strife with Death wrings power, and sea-
 soned confidence.
O'er the awakening infant, drowsing eld, and the
 mindless,
 Their individual Spirit glows enthroned in
 Heaven,
Albeit at dawn, or even, or from confusion of
 cloudland,
 Earth of their full radiance may remain bereaven:
 Yea, under God's grand eyes all souls lie pure
 and shriven.

 Nay! friend beloved! remember purple
 robes of the cavern,
 And all the wonderful dyes in dusky halls of the
 sea,
When a lucid lapse of the water lent thrills of
 exquisite pleasure,
 A tangle of living lights all over us tenderly,
When our stilly bark lay floating, or we were
 lipping the water,
 Breast to breast with the glowing, ardent heart
 of the deep!
That was a lovelier hour, whispering hope to the
 spirit,

Suspiria.

Breathing a halcyon calm, that lulled despair to
    sleep ;
Fairy flowers of the ocean, opening innermost
    wonder,
Kindle a rosy morn impearled in the waterways,
A myriad tiny diamond founts arise in the coralline,
    Anemones love to be laved in the life of the
        chrysoprase :
The happy heart of the water in many unknown
    recesses
    Childly babbled, and freely to glad companions :
We will be patient, friend, through all the moods of
    the terror,
    Waiting in solemn hope resurrection of our suns !

            Cherish loves that are left, pathetic stars
                in the gloaming ;
        Howe'er they may wax and wane, they are with
            us to the end ;
The Past is all secure, the happy hours and the
    mournful
    Involved i' the very truth of God Himself, my
        friend !
It is well to wait in the darkness for the Deliverer's
    moment,
    With a hand in the hand of God, strong Sire of
        the universe ;

It is well to work our work, with cheering tones
    for a brother,
  Whose poor bowed soul, like ours, the horrible
    gulfs immerse;
Then dare all gods to the battle! Who of them all
    may shame us?
  The very shows of the world have fleeting form
    from thee:
Discover but thy task, embrace it firm with a
    purpose;
  Find, and hold by Love, for Love is Eternity.

Sark, 1881.

    O to be sure for ever! weary of hopes
      and guesses,
  I would the film might fall that veils our orbs in
    night!
At eve grey phantom armies guard the mighty
    mountain,
  Denying free approach to wistful wondering
    sight:
A Presence dim divined through blind impalpable
    motion,
  An awful formless Form, i' the core of change
    unmoved,

Suspiria.

No more was ours, until the grand invincible
  Angel,
  The clear-eyed North blew bare Heaven's azure
    heights, and proved
Hope's heavenliest flight weak-winged ; his breath
    with clangorous challenge
  Dissolved the cloud-battalions, withering shamed
    away :
Behold, in sunrise dyed, a wondrous vision of high
    crag,
  Spires of leaping flame arrested in mid-play ;
Peak, rock-tower, and dome ; huge peals of an
    ocean of thunder
  Assumed a bodily form in yonder wild array !
And the long continuous roll of cloudy storm
    subsiding
  Was tranced to awful slopes of smooth grey
    precipice,
While over all up-soared, retiring into the heavens,
  Ever higher and higher, snows and gleaming ice!
Plain beyond plain, the strophes of a glorious
    poem,
  Voyaging stately and calm to heights of the
    argument . . . .
How to be sure for ever ? deepening all our being,
  And emptying self of self, with Truth we shall
    be blent.

Yon hierarchy sublime of calm ethereal
    mountain
Was born of earth's fierce passion, world-con-
    founding throes,
Fire, and battle, and gloom; the livid demon of
    lightning
    Flashed his zigzag blaze to be a norm for those;
Birth and death, monotonous toil in deeps of the
    ocean,
    Co-operant blind to fashion a far-off repose.
Whose brief earth-hour may taste ripe future fruit
    of the ages?
    Gauge with a life's one pace the march of the
    armies of God?
Forestall results of time, flash all the sun from a
    dew-drop?
    But where the Sire hath willed, there every foot-
    step trod.

    'Tis only a little we know; but ah! the
    Saviour knoweth;
I will lay the head of a passionate child on His
    gentle breast,
I poured out with the wave, He founded firm with
    the mountain;
    In the calm of His infinite eyes I have sought
    and found my rest.

Suspiria.

O to be still on the heart of the God we know in
    the Saviour,
Feeling Him more than all the noblest gifts He
    gave!
To be is more than to know; we near the Holy of
    Holies
In coming home to Love; we shall know beyond
    the grave.

    Ah! the peace of the beautiful realm, like
        dew, sinks into my spirit;
True and tender friend, I love to be here with
    thee.
The pines, tall fragrant columns of a magnificent
    temple,
Are ranged before the ethereal mountain majesty:
While a dove-coloured lapse of the water merrily
    murmurs a confidence
Into a quiet ear of twilit beautiful bowers;
Sweet breath of the pyrola woos us, white waxen
    elf of the woodland,
And two tired hearts may play awhile with the
    innocent flowers.

San Martino, 1882.

AUTUMN.

I.—ALONE.

LEAVES from lofty elms on high
In pale air swim shadowy;
Fall,
Till, level with a weathered wall,
Glow their autumn colours all;
Faintly rustle, touching earth;
Where, in mimicry of mirth,
With a crisper rustle dance,
When the viewless winds advance,
Driven leaves, decayed and brown,
Eddying as they are blown.
Dear illusions perish so,
Summer nurslings, ere the snow;
Loosen from a fading youth,
Leave us barren to the truth.
Nay, they blossom forth again!
Spring from winter, joy from pain,
Again!

Autumn. 93

How yon leaflet floats, returning
To the tree where leaves are burning!
Or is it a small dark bird
Nestling in the boughs unheard?
Lo! a latticed height of planes,
Green athwart blue skyey lanes,
Blue laving continents of cloud,
Violet vapour thunder-browed:
Yellowing foliage is fair,
Gold-green as an evening air,
Thronged upon a deep dove-grey;
Higher up the halls of day,
Light darkens, yet doth not consume
Boughs waving in a fiery tomb,
In a gash of brazen fire,
Early sunset's ruddy pyre.

II.—LOVERS ON THE RIVER.

Floating on a slender river,
A pale violet flame,
Windless air, a violet flame,
Clear reflections only quiver,
Flickering with margin blurred!
Whisper, bird,
A word!

Through a mossy arch impearled,
Rounded in the water-world,
Love! behold a little boat,
With a white sail, stilly float
Far off, even
In Heaven;
For the river-reach appears
To mount a violet air;
A spirit's wings in violet air,
Free from human woes and fears,
In our dreams
It seems!
While yon kine upon the marge,
On the meadowy marge,
Greenly-glowing pasture large,
Send their gleam of coloured shadow
Beyond a green bank from the meadow,
Where rushes are,
Afar!
Perished all sweet summer posies;
Yet a radiant air
Lavishes more fair
Roseflush from windwoven roses
Rich and rare.
Now we float in orchard closes,
Darkly, magically green,
Ne'er an apple seen:
Till the water winds between

Beechen hills,
And leaf-fed rills,
Whose rich furnace chestnut-gold
Dowers the wave with wealth untold ;
Flakes of burning gold
Lying on the vivid grass
Gorgeous, while we softly pass.
Lo ! slim aspens yellow-pale,
Inlaying far mist while we sail :
Whisper, bird,
A word !
Whisper, murmur, never move
From thy pillow, love !
From my bosom, tender dove !
Lying quiet, hand in hand,
We will dream we need not land
Upon the shore,
Where evermore
Love, a rainbow, dear illusion,
Melts into the world's confusion !
We will dream no chance may sever
Two fond hearts upon the river
Of their own felicity !
We will dream Love need not die ;
Only fly,
In the even,
To Heaven !

III.—IN THE GLENS.

Upon the huge rock-rooted elm we stood,
That hangs and murmurs o'er a shadowy deep,
Where a dim glen lies silently in sleep.
There one tall ash, crowned queen of all the wood,
Rises above a labyrinthine brood,
Verdurous underglooms, adown the steep
Riverward falling : nightdews well and weep
In their rich bowers of odorous solitude.
Boulders block leafy cataracts, that brave
With rebel surge the crag's commanding wall :
Beeches burn brilliant against a grave
Mist-sombred russet foliage, that all
Seems, like a surf, to mount the steep, nor fall;
Climbs the high cliffs, a never-refluent wave.

We swung beneath the rugged antlered form ;
Clambering, plunged into a green profound,
Ash-pale rent vapours gathering around
Those vast elm-arms upwrithen to the storm ;
Till we beheld a cliff's grey bulk enorm,
Crimson beyond the woodland where we wound,
Whose boughs half veiled the grandeur sunset-
    warm ;
High cliff that doth the tidal Avon bound.

Autumn.

Here, where steep rocks are riven abrupt and gory,
Where leans, weird thyrsus, a thin branchless tree,
Ivied, discrowned, athwart their promontory,
Midmost all rank and fleshy growths that be,
Nightshade, worn tumbled stones, and trunks mist-hoary,
Satyrs and fauns may hold strange revelry!

Then we emerged upon a slumbering tide,
Where sounding fire-ships to the populous port
Draw vessels laden; there white birds resort,
Whom light discovers, or hill-shadows hide,
While slowly in aërial maze they glide.
Gorgeous Autumn holds her stately court,
A solemn queen, like Tragedy; gold-wrought,
Her train fills all the glens; she is Death's bride;
For soon she shall be robed in a white shroud.
But we, fond friends, we dared to breathe aloud
Vows of a love undying; though a cloud
Gathered, passed over, melted in the blue;
Though withering worlds, like leaves, around us flew;
And all the abysses yawned upon us two.

All awful Forces of the Universe,
Within, beneath, around us, and above,
Dark armoured Phantoms, frowned upon our love,

Breathing cold scorn thereover, for a curse.
Behold! how blind wild hurricanes disperse
A foam-flake, inland blown from a sea-cove;
So man's fair hopes inviolable prove.
Cling, hearts, a moment ere the gulfs immerse!
For Self, and Sin, with all that sundereth,
Mad Chance, and Change, faint Absence, and dim Death,
A ghostly army, leagued against Love's breath,
Have sworn to annihilate; life's shadows close:
But Love, whose blossom fleeteth as it blows,
Rests in the heart of a Divine repose.

MONTE ROSA.

Rosa! thy battlement of beaming ice
Burns, like the battlement of Paradise!
One block of long white light unsulliable
Glows in deep azure, Heaven's cathedral wall,
Gleams, a pure loveliness of angel thought,
With Heaven's inviolable ardour fraught.
A myriad flowers play fearless at thy feet,
And many a flying fairy sips their sweet,
While with the Sun of souls, the Paraclete,
Thou communest up yonder, rapt from earth,
Robed in the evening-gold, or morning-mirth.
One cloudy surge from thy tremendous steep
Recoils, and hangs a warder o'er thy sleep,
Whose awful spirit in deep reverie
Above the world abides eternally:
While seraphs roam around thy silver slope,
Nestle in thy hollows, and with fair-flying hope
Temper the intolerable severity
Of holiest Purpose; many a floweret blows
In the unearthly Honour of thy snows,

Monte Rosa.

Like innocent loves in souls erect, sublime,
Who breathe above the tainted air of time:
While many a falling water kisses
Tinkling emerald abysses
Of shadowy cavern with cool rain,
Clear gliding rills in polished porcelain
Channels descending o'er a crystal plain
From the Frost-Spirit's palace bowers
Of sea-green pinnacles, and toppling towers,
And grim white bastion defiled
With rocky ruin of the wild:
While over all thy luminous pure ice
Rears the stupendous radiant precipice,
High terraces the seraphim have trod,
Stairs dwindling fainter, as they near the abode,
Where in light unimaginable dwells God.

But now around thee sullen, murmuring Storm
Flings his dark mantle; such around the form
Of awful Samuel, summoned from the tomb,
At Endor rose: then all is rayless gloom
About thy Presence for a little while;
Until God draws in His cathedral aisle
The folding shroud from thy dread countenance.
Behold! above the storm, as in a trance,
Thy grand, pale Face abides, regarding us,
As from Death's realm afar, like risen Lazarus!

Monte Rosa.

Isled in dusk blue, one star thrills faintly shining
Over thy crest in mournful day's declining:
Far away glens deep solitary blanch
With snow fresh fallen of the avalanche;
Forested prowls the haggard wolf, the craven,
While o'er me croaking weirdly wheels the raven;
Yonder in twilight, fretted with fierce fire,
Lower vast vans of hungering lammergeyer!
Dark vassal crags, who guard thine awful throne,
Wearing dim forests for a sounding zone,
Divide to let thy torrent coursers flee
With thunderous embassage to the great Sea.
   Behold! on grand long summits bowed
A huge ghost-cataract of cloud!
Niagara motionless, unvoiced,
In dim rapt air portentous poised!
But ruffled plumes of Tempest lower
Where the giant cliffs uptower,
While their impregnable fort frowns
Defiant, and their haughty crowns
Their vapoury veils,
Livid ice-ribs, and wolf-fanged teeth
Threaten implacable with death
Rash mortal who assails!
Beneath them the heart fails.
One rayless wilderness of stone
Upreared, they warn from their bleak throne;

Ruined halls of lonely storms,
Whose are weird dishevelled forms,
Dark as eerie crags that loom,
Brooding haggard in the gloom,
Assuming semblance of rent thunder,
While they wait expectant under.

Lo! one wide ocean of tumultuous sound
Terrific bursts! flooding Heaven's profound,
Shatters the concave! hark! how, one by one,
Each monarch mountain on his far white throne,
Shocked, buffeted by that infernal word,
His own portentous utterance hath roared,
Tearing night, startled with flame-sweep of sword,
And bellowing fierce frantic wrath
Into the steam of that hell-broth
Around: white fires flash swift unfurled
Over dim ruin of a watery world!
Hark! huge war-standards ponderous unrolling
Over wild surges of tempestuous blast!
While storm-stifled bells are tolling
For souls of pilgrims who have passed
Home at last!
But here amid earthquaking shocks,
Whirlwinds rave around the rocks:
Great pines, agonizing horrent
O'er the white terror of the torrent,

In wild lightning-fits leap out
From death's womb, a ghostly rout,
And all wild demon-chariots roll,
Hurtling, chaotic, blind, reft from control;
Until the elemental rage subsides;
Ebbs the fell fury of ethereal tides;
Atlantic billows of slow sullen sound
Subsiding wander o'er the immeasurable Profound.

. . . . Rosa! the Moon soothes thine unearthly rest,
And Peace pervades the snows upon thy breast!

Val Anzasca.

TO ERIC FROM THE ALPS.

The fragrant pines are green, love,
    The pines are fair and tall,
Dear is the Alpine scene, love,
    Peak, flower, and waterfall;
But my heart's tendrils favour
    Humbler pines at home,
For there the weak feet waver,
    That never learned to roam.
One day about the wood, dear,
    Thy steps began to go,
And all my stony mood, dear,
    Was moved to happy flow;
But when they ceased from pleasure
    Upon the woodland floor,
Silence in deeper measure
    Than e'er was known before
Returned for evermore, dear,
    Returned for evermore.

IN THE DOLOMITES.

ONE haughty, precipitous peak, enveloped, embraced in a white cloud,
   Hath freed himself from the clasp, and flung the cloud into space ;
A woman, I deem, once loved ! now all uncrowned and degraded,
   She lies a white heap dishevelled, not too far from his face.
Later I looked, and lo ! at his iron feet she hath grovelled,
   The cloud-bride cannot believe she is thrown for ever away !
Hath she not lain in his bosom ? all for the fault of a moment !
   The stern crag heeds her not, relentless facing the day.

MELCHA.[6]

I.

MANY have longed for a maiden fair,
Who still is free as summer air:
Longing youths are strong and bright;
She is free as summer light.
"Melcha, Melcha," parents say,
"Time flies, my child! no more delay!
Young Geraldine would lead thee home;
Worthier wooer will not come."
Half her young heart may playful lean
To the love of the love of Geraldine;
But little she cares for rout or ball,
With flushing face and soft footfall;
She plies her needle, churns her cream,
Milks a heifer of snowy gleam,
And more than all the pensive child
Loves to wander alone and wild,
With her own kindred bee or bird,
Far from all the human herd,
Over heather, over hill,
By the torrent, by the still

Melcha.

Lake-margin, in a noonday trance,
Brooding over old romance.

Melcha favours with her love
Every flowery nook and cove ;
Floats upon the placid stream,
Silvern as a silver bream,
Flying from a common life
All too full of soil and strife ;
Till once her shallop drifted to a cave
That looks upon Lough Lean's cool whispering wave,
Where silent water-light for loving eyes
Weaves mazy melodies
Over pellucid filmy fern,
Whose is many a fairy urn,
Festooning fair the rocky cavern-wall,
And glowing in a trickling waterfall,
Among sweet closely-woven mosses,
Where a rainbow globelet crosses
Ever to supply the losses,
Growing from long ferny nerves,
Like a meteor,
Startling merrily upon a flowery floor
A blue-eyed blossom, till it thrills and swerves !
 Ruddied with the fiery globe,
Autumn's gorgeous golden robe

Involves majestic mountain forms,
Crags familiar with storms,
Grandly towering a-glow,
Burning tranquil waves below,
Purpled here with miles of heather,
Shadowed often altogether.
Yonder shines the Eagle's Nest
In a glorious verdure-vest:
She hath climbed his rocky crest;
Seen the stately eagle hover,
Imperial-poised, a thunder-cloud above her,
Whom a pearly sunbeam found
Luminous-brown, with all around
Opal air, and o'er the glens
Under, and o'er all the fens.

    If eagles are monarchs of air,
        Red deer are lords of the glen!
    Behold! a stag over there,
        Defiant of hounds and men,
    In a lair of tall Osmunda,
    Antlered, large-eyed, a wonder.

    She looked upon the luminous lake,
Seeing tufts of bilberry shake
In a wandering breeze
O'er their images;
Red-boled luxuriant arbute-trees,

Melcha.

With white flower and crimson fruit,
Glossy-leavèd lave their root,
Darkening all the glass;
Saw the languid lake-lives waver
Below in a luminous water-quaver,
Where shadowy fishes pass;
Heard the lapping wavelets kiss,
While she dreamed of that or this—
Dreamed of old romance,
While light elf-like droppings dance,
Twinkling play
In a fairy spray.
"I would fly the vulgar toil;
I would fly the strife and soil;
I would slumber, and awake
In the bosom of the lake!"
She is lulled to sweet repose
By a far-off mellow chime,
By the water's murmured rhyme,
By the wild bee in the thyme,
Till her eye-lids close.
    Hark! a long sweet note resounding,
From the mountain clear rebounding!
Hills are all alive with voices,
With soft spirit noises.
Naiads of the shadowy water,
Every gentle woodland daughter,

All ye lovely fays who are
In the valleys of Glenâa !
All who haunt the Purple Mountain,
Souls of many a far-off fountain,
All in air, or underground,
Or in hollow cliff spellbound,
Breathe your delicate spirit-voices !
Eagle's Nest is all alive,
As though he were a fairies' hive ;
Musically ruffled he rejoices ;
Hurrying notes in sweet confusion,
Marrying with soft collusion ;
Awful, solemn-toned, and loud ;
Low as from beneath a shroud ;
Pausing now for a reply
From far crags and cliffs that lie
Underneath another sky !
Now they fall to slumber, murmuring un-
    quietly.
High Carantuohil is the last to hear,
Murmuring from his cloud, and solitary sphere.

What is the mild mystic trouble,
Where in the lake
Sun floats, a flashing double ?
Maiden, awake !

Melcha.

One emerges from the flood,
A snowy steed and rider, with pure radiance
    imbued!
He doth not seem of mortal mould,
Whose lineaments, how grave and pale!
Beam from a raisèd visor of gold,
Whose silver dripping mail,
And lofty plume him tall reveal
More than all sons of mortals; his white steed
Stately paces the blue mead.
Slowly toward fair Melcha's nook
His majestic course he took:
Delighted wonder made her start;
Fearless flutters her young heart.
" So my long-fondled tales are true:
Here is Lord O'Donoghue!"
He, swift leaping from his horse,
Seized her hand with gentle force:
She, gazing in the awful eyes,
Found them full of loving light;
Lovely seemed to her the knight;
Then she veiled her maiden eyes;
And her tender heart was taken,
Taken ere she was aware,
By the spirit tall and white,
Ere he spake, " O maiden fair!"
Spake with accent soft and rare,

"Wilt thou wed the waters blue?
Wilt thou love O'Donoghue?
Wilt thou love me, maiden mild?
Fair my dwelling, gentle child!
Under the blue water!
Yet, 'tis weird, and vast, and cold;
I desire a mortal daughter
To enfold!
But I know not if the wave
Unto thee would prove a grave: . . . . .
. . . . All those wonders shall be thine,
If thou wilt be mine!"
"Thine!"
So the little Melcha breathed;
And the spirit's arms enwreathed
Her a moment, as he won her:
"Darling, meet me when May morning,
Earth with bridal wreaths adorning,
Opens earliest eyes upon her!
Wait me on the tufted rock:
Well thou knowest I will not mock . . . .
. . . . From your white bosom give me yon
 silk scarf like flame!"
He stole it, she allowing, and he vanished as
 he came.

Melcha.

O ! how poor is our dull earth,
Till the happy morn have birth.
And Melcha's father's bitter wife
Doth not sweeten Melcha's life !
With such unearthly eyes she moved, it roused
    a dark derision ;
She stumbled o'er her daily tasks i' the
    glamour of her vision.
She moved as one who is amazed,
With a sudden splendour dazed:
" Dare I with a spirit go
To the crystal realms below ?
And will he keep faith with me,
Far lowlier than he ?
I deem he was a monarch mild ;
And yet a Paynim, I a Christian child !
May I wed a fairy undefiled ?
But he is glorious and true !
I told the priest of our sweet interview,
Under close confession-seal :
He deemed it some hallucination ;
' Our Lady hover over thee, and heal !
Flee very verges of damnation !
I know thou dost prefer thy nook
By yonder lake to holy book,
Or holy ordinance ; be wary !
Dally not with Paynim fairy !'

Nay, my love's a holy feast!
He but dotes, our aged priest:
And since I know he must be good,
I will tell him of the rood!
What a noble conquest this!
He shall taste eternal bliss,
By his love for little me;
And, for reward, what wonders he
Will reveal to my glad mind,
By the many undivined!
Yet do I sleep, or do I wake?
Shall I live beneath the lake? . . .
He told me 'twas like Heaven there . . .
With him I will fly anywhere!"

But Melcha had a younger sister,
Whom she cherished; and she kissed her
With strange tenderness that night
Of April, ere the eventful light.
Misting tears are in her eyes,
Looking on her ere she flies;
Looking in toward the bed,
Where a fair and dreamless head
Slumbers on without a sorrow,
Blithe to-day, and blithe to-morrow.
Little Melcha cannot sleep.
Shall she laugh, or shall she weep?

Melcha.

She must leave her virgin chamber,
Where she taught a rose to clamber ;
She must leave her little bird,
Who in a sweet May dawn is stirred,
And the snowy folds of fume,
That curtain frail her beamy room,
Yea, and leave the mother's grave,
Her young grief was wont to lave.

Ere the sun she flies away :
Is it not the first of May ?
But she hath a favourite fawn
Silver-clear as a May dawn ;
Tho' he must leave her at the lake,
Till the last he'll not forsake !
Still a silver twinkling star
Laughs over woodlands of Glenâa ;
Yet the merry bird hath warbled
O'er his five eggs wine-immarbled,
Notes that fall a rich perfume
Over orchards in white bloom ;
These festoon a violet air,
As she looks among the boughs,
In her bridal gossamer,
Where no costly jewel glows,
Save some dews that fall on her
From young foliage and fir.

Now a rosy gleam hath tinged
Waters fair, and forest-fringed ;
Far away tall Carantuohil
Glows in Heaven, a lonely jewel !
There a moment let her falter,
There before the woodland altar,
Where a lamp for ever burns
In a chapel among the ferns,
Asking of the carven Christ :
"Do I well to keep the tryst ?"

  She is at the tufted rock,
Hearing gentle water shock
Clear beneath her ; a careering hawk
Hangs o'er abrupt dark-wooded heights of
  Torc !
At whose rich feet tall ash, hawthorn, and
  holly,
Hang shadowy bowers over waters melancholy.
Dinis isle, and many an isle,
Fair await the morning smile ;
Between the hills a purple light fills heavenly
  chalices ;
Till lo ! the Sun Himself enthroned in
  mountain palaces !

  And when He touched the flashing flood,
Music welled from wave and wood ;

A celestial harmony
Floated over earth and sky. . . .
While from burning waves of blue
Burst the spirit O'Donoghue!
Beautiful youths and maidens, lovely water-
    powers,
All enwreathed with heavenly flowers,
Like airy fancies from a poet's bowers,
Undulating o'er the gay
Crystal glory, many a fay,
Follow the war-horse as he prances,
Foam dancing all around him as he dances!
She beholds her crimson scarf
In the beams of morning laugh,
Bound about her stately charmer,
Bound about his radiant armour—
Now they are near the trysting-place;
Melcha's heart is like a leaf;
But when her lover looks into her face,
Those glorious amorous eyes are her relief.
He opens wide his arms to take her!
She will dare the fatal leap!
From his alluring nought shall shake her. . .
She hath plunged into the deep! . . .
And the fairy fawn must weep.
Held to his heart she dares the dive;
Explores a waterworld alive!

Only a vapour seems to glide,
Where O'Donoghue won his bride!

II.

How shall a mortal dare to tell
What there the little maid befell?
Nought she knows within the grasp,
Save that it is her lover's clasp. . . .
Released, she finds herself in wondrous
    columned halls,
Whose grand infinitude her slender soul
    appals.
Many a water-green, self-luminous column
Stupendous rises in dim heights and solemn.
Their labyrinths for evermore extend
In hollow-echoing chambers with no end.
Self-luminous are they, and yet very dim:
She turns, and hides her timid face in him.
"Is it not splendid, love, my water-dwelling?
With spheral music all around thee welling?
My rainbow pillars, glowing with soft light,
Soaring till lost in Heaven's infinite?"
"Alas!" she said, "I hear low sounds unlinked;
Nor seem your columns with blithe colours
    tinct.

For all is sombre-hued, though beautiful.
Alas! my hearing and mine eyes are dull!"
"Nay, come, for thou art dazzled!" he replied,
In gentle tones of love to his young bride;
Then bore her over the dim-shining floor
To where climbed, like a giant conqueror,
One of the columns, faintly tinged with rose.
"Melcha! behold! how glorious it glows!
Here, with the rose-hue, hues of the young apple,
And of young pear leaves, blend, as by the chapel
Near your sweet home, my love; and violet,
With many other flower souls, have met,
Soft interchanging delicate qualities,
Alliance and imminglement of dyes.
They ever move with music from beneath,
Flower souls to bloom in many a fragrant wreath
Up yonder, in your visible world of light;
But here in mine they are married ere the flight.
Ever the Life from caverned gloom swift flushes,
Mantling, as though through stalks of water-rushes,
Here through these columns in your world to blossom,
Innumerably fair from Night's own bosom.
Now these have changed to a wave of breezy ocean,
Now to a river of full mazy motion;
Here clouds arise, their hearts relieved in rain;
Here two young forms, ere beauty's blossom wane
Clasp one another in pure loveliness;

Here treachery murders, feigning a caress:
All genders a confused, life-labouring sound,
As Vulcan wrought in stithys underground.
Here element to element fond hies,
Or with a hatred of repulsion flies,
Each following his own affinities.
The rhythmic molecule, that only moves,
Foreknows blithe genius, who sings and loves;
Crystal snowflower, albumen ocean-floor,
Are faint foreshadowing of cells, and more,
Hold in their womb alcyon, moss, or rose;
Yea, rosier virgins lovelier than those!
There yawns no blank unfathomable abysm
Between the man, the sunbeam, and the prism!
Heaving impartial, Night engendereth
Genius crowned, and Love with rosy wreath;
Madness all haggard; bloody Hate; pale Death;
Or Sun, and Moon, and Stars, whose semblance dim
With man, and beast, and bird of shadowy limb,
Follow in bewildering swift change;
All into one another find free range;
Yet, save the flower-souls, they all appear
As in their embryo, phantasmal here."

But Melcha very faintly may discern
Those ardours, even where they brightly burn,
Needing some sweet assistance of his eyes:
So to another column-stalk he flies.

Here he revealed the bowels of old Earth;
Fire, and slow water-growths, and many a birth
Forgotten, long bereft of grief or mirth.
There, in a third, intolerably royal,
A soul of Sunlight bursteth, while the loyal
Planets obeisant with their moons are moving;
Systems through solitary spaces roving
In primal order, while young nebulæ
Blindly brood over worlds of grief and glee.
While these are clearest glories, yet there follow
All most prevailing in a sister hollow.
There follow faintly other forms and colours,
Herbs, and live things with many joys and dolours.
For every magic column hath a class
Of powers prevailing in his mystic glass:
This towering droops with wealth of many a world,
Like some vast palm, whose boughs are night-impearled,
Or richly laden with dates' golden clusters;
So fountainous in ether float the starry lustres;
Even as a Geyser, or a fountain shoots
In one straight water from perennial roots;
Falls in blue air with myriad diamonds fair hurled.
    In yet another pillar he discovers
Swarming low lives; the animal world; with lovers;
Shadowy presentment of fair youths and maidens,
Lovingly marrying in fresh flowering aidenns;

With little babes, who laughing reach soft arms
To where above them mother's eyelight warms ;
All roseate dissolving ; pale wild-eyed
Faces of saint, or seeker ; there harsh Pride,
Horror, and Shame ; there Lust, and Cruelty
Deformed arise in mists of lurid dye.
Here springs the growth supreme of Good and Evil,
Twin-birth indissoluble : angel, devil,
Eternal hierachies infinite,
Animal, human ; sorrow and delight
Issue in morning-gold, or sanguine gloom,
From one divine unfathomable Womb ;
Neither, and both, and more than both ; the Whole,
Adored in silence of the fainting soul.
Hearken ! a sound of restless-hearted ocean ;
Or of a city's far-off heard emotion !
  But little Melcha shrinking hides in him.
" I faint !" she cries, "for though mine eyes be dim,
I cannot bear these awful sights and sounds,
Where all immingling my poor sense confounds."
    " Nay, here," he chaunted, her own demon lover,
While in his arms more loosely he enwove her,
" Here in solemn halls of Thought,
The marvel of the World is ever wrought !
Famine, a vulture, glares on men to ruin brought ;

Here loud volcanoes whelm with fiery lava ;
Sin desolates a groaning earth with blood ;
Here men and women loll by mango and lush guava ;
Fair Bacchanals are reeling near a winy wave or wood ;
Yea! and the Man Divine dies for alien good."
    " Ah!" she exclaimeth, "where is then the Rood ?
I lose my Lord in your sublime turmoil!
Not so I learned Him on my native soil."
    " Yet is He here in heavenlier raiment dressed ;
More nobly than in your old forms expressed !
But now behold! for thou must needs admire
Monuments wrought, as though from living fire!
Among these columns rising into real
Stand fair enchantments of Thought's own ideal :
And lo ! among them, wandering pale-browed,
Mighty creators, with raised eyes or bowed,
Silently brooding, clothed in solemn cloud !
Here at a Plato's, or a Newton's gaze,
To luminous order from a nebulous haze
Gleams many a column : here Spinoza wanders
Schelling, the Stagyrite, or Hegel, ponders ;
Kepler, or Galileo, crowned with stars ;
All Hero-shatterers of prison bars ;
Columbus, and our earth-discoverers :

Eagle-eyed martyrs of the quest for truth,
Whose effort bloometh in immortal youth :
Men dowered with the world's rank insult and hot hate,
Because they dared to smite our swollen state,
Whose idol-wheels a human blood must lubricate!
Tyndale, Mazzini, Regulus, or Tell ;
And they who by the Malian water fell !
Cato, and Manlius ; patriots who died ;
Harmodius, and all who brave a tyrant's purple pride !
Gems in the crown of Freedom set ;
Washington, or Lafayette !
Here walks the wisest of Athenian teachers,
And here the mightiest of Hebrew preachers ;
Founders of all the commonwealths of earth ;
Founders from whom world-shadowing faiths have birth.
Moses, Mohammed, with the Indian :
Beethoven, Angelo, or Titian . . . . . .
Whose spirit stalks alone ? the worldworn man,
Florentine Dante ! he the third grand ghost,
Who seems to rise above the glorious host
Of Dædal poets—third—there are two others ;
Homer, with Avon's bard ; and yet some brothers
Have scarce a lowlier post, from Orient
And western climes ; they form of sound, or stone,

Or metal, colour, word, a monument,
Wherein their own essential selves have grown.
Perishing sea-lives leave the coral-forest
Fair from their hearts; like these on whom thou
    porest;
And glory of the rainbow-rippled shells
Flows from a lowly life that ever wells.
Luxuriant labyrinths of sound are floated
From choirs of viewless harmonists full-throated !
Rearers of Temples, and Cathedrals grand,
Whom earth remembers not, imperial band,
Behold ! with Pheidias, and Praxiteles;
And many who left no memory with these."
But when the Knight beheld some members of the
    throng,
Impetuously he burst forth into song :

" Builders of the warning tower,
Whose flashing eye commands the storm,
When thunderous wild waves fling foaming arms
    of power,
To hurl below, to shatter, the tall Saviour form !
Fathers of fire-souled mechanic
Demons whirlwind-limbed are ye;
Of wrought-iron tubes Titanic,
Thrown 'thwart rivers, and the free
Heretofore unfettered sea !

"Armoured monsters on the deep,
Grim whale-like islands, formidably sleep:
Your resolute fire-ships throbbing sweep!
I' the teeth of howling solid blasts,
And billowy cataracts hoar ocean casts
To overwhelm, ye find the Pole,
Guard a world-wide empire whole;
Quell the foes of freedom with indomitable soul!
  "Sensitive needle in a crystal shrine,
Who dost, like Conscience, evermore incline
Toward one Eternal Pole, although the cloud
From storm-tossed mariner His radiance shroud!
By thee Gama dares to round
Afric's awful utmost bound!
And the Genoese discovers
A morning-land for Liberty's blithe lovers!
  "Your magic glass reveals a realm
Too far, too fine, for human eyes!
While suns, and planets, and fair moons o'erwhelm,
In fairy-like societies,
Under our feet, in our own frames,
One organizing Reason flames!
Man shrinks abashed within his shell,
Abashed by atom, world, and cell;
Yet magnifies the mighty Mind,
Subtler than light, more swift than wind,
That tangles in Her ordered prisms

Rays of unvoyageable abysms,
Pulsing a million years through strange illimitable
    places,
Hurled from hot hearts of stars, far homes of un-
      imaginable races!
  "Iron-souled Inventors, you
Are of earth's illustrious few!
Conquerors of reluctant Nature,
Adding to man's pigmy stature;
With delver's lamp, and axe, and power-loom,
Your spirit broods upon the gloom;
Ye have arisen
To irradiate the serfs' dull prison!
Ye are they who forge the chain,
Flashing thought from brain to brain,
Not to bind,
But liberate mankind!
Ye have winged the fiery dragon,
Thundering to feast or drouth,
Ye who pass life's foaming flagon
Tumultuously from mouth to mouth,
Rushing North and rushing South!
Who devastate with rumbling tumbril-wheel,
Rifle, cannon, shell, or steel,
Human frames, and human hearts;
While our wharves, and all our marts
Glow wealthier from your arts:

With hideous scurf, with lurid smoke unblest,
Ye devastate earth's flowery rest,
Her virginal sweet vest !
Life's a journey ;
Life's a tourney ;
Swift we go !
Hail ! wild wind of our strong speed,
Lightning, and a clangorous thunder !
Farm or village, town or mead,
Flashing past, earth trembles under ;
Autumn leaves about us twirling,
Tumultuous clouds around us whirling,
Ringing axles eager to burst forth in flame !
Who shall tame us ?
Praise or blame us !
Shrieking onward,
Hurrying sunward,
Swift we go,
Reeling, jarring, or with crash of horrible overthrow,
Darkly travelling, ever nearing yonder Orient
    aglow !"

  Some ghosts, in gazing on a crystal tower,
Where man, or animal, or herb, or flower
More dominates, or sea, or earth, or sun,
Convert the several Powers they gaze upon

To gods of aspect glorious and strange,
Bewraying each his nature in the change;
Benign now; now malevolent they range.

And Melcha saw some spirits wandering there,
Whose bodies yet abode i' the upper air.
Her lover, he who disappeared from earth
By other portals than Death's mystic birth
Into an alien land, so silent seeming;
As stars seem silent, or dim forests teeming
With infinite fairy-like societies,
Whose rich life-dramas we may faint surmise;
Her lover, he may view the spirits moving,
And she by him; but earthly souls, in roving
Through the stupendous halls that never end,
Perceive not those who died, although they wend
Their ways beside them, nor some beings nigh
Of another order in the hierarchy.
It may be few perceive them; yet all here
Assemble, each from his own natal sphere.
Only a dweller in a foreign star
Hath his more wonted haunts from these afar;
In other realms of Nature's laboratory.
Nor of the dead may all distinguish well
Their dead companions; for souls from hell,
And souls from heaven mutually repel.
But all seems peopled with impalpable pale hosts,

A common crowd, and even with less than human ghosts.
No word is breathed between the shapes who wander:
On one another's work they reverently ponder;
Knowing the Lord all over it and under.
The wisest ask no homage for their names,
To One all-bounteous yielding private claims.
And where some organizing thought, long gleaming
Upon a column's core, hath left it beaming,
For ever after, when a follower gazes,
Reason's high hallowing remains, and blazes
I' the core of these enchanted chrysoprases.

  The lovers first behold a Dædal thought,
With the world's buoyant youth sublimely fraught.
Here, as in purest marble white,
Though with a sunrise faintly flushing,
Are nobly-moulded forms who fight,
Chariots and steeds to battle rushing.
Here glorious Achilles mourns his friend,
Embracing a young warrior's corse,
While, with head bowed to earth, each generous horse
Of race divine who brought him mourns Patroclus' end.
There Hector flies the avenging Champion,
Roused from his sullen rest upon the plain;

Thrice round Troy-ramparts, by Achilles slain,
Lashed to his car, before proud Ilion,
Her hero, with most cruel contumely,
Is dragged, in sight of poor Andromache.

 Odysseus, deemed long dead, clad in rude
  weeds,
Growling low in his lion soul, yet feeds
With little insolent men beneath the dome
Pertaining to him, his ancestral home :
They dare his queen, and his young heir offend :
But now he draws the bow none save himself can
  bend ;
And while they cower, divining the dread end,
Throws off concealment, towers in his own hall,
And turns the twanging death upon them all !

 A kind of mighty pedestal upholds
This living imagery with green folds,
As were they heavings of an emerald ocean,
Ever young, resonant with stormful motion.

 Further, as on a mass of diamond,
Some figures of colossal port arise,
With tragic face and form ; fixed by a bond
Of art inviolable their mournful guise
Of guilt and agony ; they seem to glow
Darkly as bronze late molten, or like some
Whelmed in fire-floods of Herculaneum.

Hangs the god-Titan, hurling scorn at Jove,
Torn by Heaven's ravening bird, implacable in
    love.

There generous-hearted Œdipus, who mocks
Sinister breathings of impending doom,
Staggers beneath accumulating shocks
Of Destiny Divine; then bows in gloom,
As a brave man with youthful strength adorned
Yields to a purple smothering Simoom,
Or snowy whirlwinds, that he blithely scorned
At morning on a mountain;
                    here Antigone
Supports her father blind; there one with lavish
    locks,
Her brother slain, entombs, defying tyranny;
Perishing in her youth with splendid piety.

"These works are wonderful," avowed the
    bride,
"I love to explore their glories with my love;
But I should tremble if I left your side——"
"Nay, thou shalt be at home here, O my dove!
Even as one of us—once more behold
What marvel yonder chasm may unfold!"

A lurid haze upsteams from an Abyss,
Immense, profound, down-narrowing gradual:
There, as in ruby wrought, souls reft of bliss

Agonize all around the furnace wall,
Clean-carven in relief, as on a gem
Blood red; so one grim thought hath imaged them.
And lo! that awful Shade himself stood nigh
Gazing abstracted, with dread light upon
His haggard features: then he raised his face;
And those two lovers noted the full grace
Of all the seer, with Beatrice by,
Beheld in Heaven, where spirits who have won
Their crown of glory form a snow-white rose,
Ethereal jewels; every petal glows
Beamingly loving, or their ardours cluster
To a mighty eagle of empyreal lustre,
And to a Cross immense; aloft they noted those.

"Now let us pause," the mortal urges; "all
My brain reels with the marvels that appal,
How fair soever!" the Knight folding her,
A grateful shade involved them, and they sank
In one another's arms, with no demur
From either lover:
            When they woke from slumber,
When loving eyes of hers the lovelight drank
From his wild orbs, did any sorrow cumber
Their lakelike splendour?—but he sighed and said:
"To a strange bridegroom thou in sooth art wed!
Even in my Pagan monarchy of old,

No letter of a priestly creed might hold
My soul, who will her ample wings unfold.
Yet ere Christ's Planet in the Orient rose,
Justly and wisely did I rule my land,
Yonder on earth ; till my rapt words disclose,
One sunny eve within my castle hall,
(Lapping its portal silver waters doze)
The phantom Future, whose far-off footfall
Mine ears prophetic on faint-sounding sand
Of present time laid listening discern.
And while the chiefs around all hearkening burn
With inspiration of my words, I rise,
And seem to vanish from their wondering eyes
Within the waters of our tranquil lake.
Mightier rulers follow in my wake ;
A Faith Diviner, subtler joys and woes ;
Yet ever more my wistful longing grows
For some dear feminine heart to dwell with me
Here in Thought's own profound tranquillity.
I want a fresh, a guileless Christian spirit
To breathe an ampler, a diviner air,
Than in her lowly cell she may inherit ;
So mine imperial burden one may share,
And faithful Love's unshamed simplicity
Direct the challenge of keen Reason's eye.
So I make more, and purify my pleasure,
By halving our unfathomable treasure.

"In summer, or in stormier weather,
We will explore God's wondrous worlds together.
How often have I failed to baffle wrong,
Because thou wast not nigh to make me strong!
Wrestling with loathsome coils about me prest,
How oft the mortal Hydra mocked my rest!
One withering glance of thine had scotched the
  Pest!
Shall not a child from our two selves be born,
Who shall annihilate Error with blithe scorn?
And yet, alas! I doubt if thou canst breathe
Freely in these my realms: they leave thee pale
  with death!"

"Nay, I will strive to help thee, and to live:
I chose thee: I have dared the dimlit dive!
And yet, in sooth, my spirit seems confused
As one who, falling far, lies dazed and bruised.
I only fear lest, from my native sphere
Deserting, I may find no haven here!"

Lo! living mimes of all the human drama!
Swift shifting scenes of life's weird panorama!
Silent succeeding groups of figures gathered
From forth dim air, and slowly vanishing:
In various forms all these the semblance bring
Of very men and women, yet are fathered
Of human Art, not nature; all are moulded,

So that their inner being lies unfolded
In many a moment of concentrate life,
Wherewith their mutual-moving moods are rife.

    By night, upon the rock-built platform standing,
Hamlet hath heard the sire's dread shade commanding;
Unwilling scattereth his life-love-blossom,
Whose sweet shed petals flutter in his bosom:
Here in her haunted room adjures the mother;
Here wrestles desolate, alone with fury-fates that smother:
Till smiting down the evil with a tardy random doom,
He and the innocent sink with them in the same dull tomb!

    There a fiend-woman with red hand upbraids
The lingering manhood, that so swiftly fades
Under Hell's own exorcism, when the twain
Their royal reverend guest have foully slain,
Who slept the just man's sleep beneath their roof:
And there Macbeth's dyed soul is put to proof,
When at the banquet rises a pale ghost,
To upbraid the horror-faced usurping host.

    With Romeo on her heart young Juliet,
In Love's own garden, swears no morning yet

Melcha.

Troubles the cool blue air of summer night,
Or moon, or stars, or Philomel's delight!
That was no lark-note! bird of envious morn! . . .
Death meets them, and all lovers, with his chilling
    scorn!

    Further, wild laughter in stained lips and eyes,
Fat Falstaff, full of merry jests and lies,
Carouses with a prince of generous blood,
Where in Old London a quaint tavern stood.

    Cordelia implores her poor mad Lear
To know her for his faithful-hearted child,
Nor longer do her wrong; he cannot clear
In his dark mind, all shattered and defiled
By traitor cruelty, reflect her love,
Once in his own blind arrogance reviled:
And when she dawns within his soul, the dove
Death sneering snatches from him; he may moan,
Yearning remorseful for her—she is gone.
All lost to love and light, he may but die . . .
So, cursing, laughing, weeping, passes Life's grim
    pageantry.

    Behold! what seems the ruin of the Past,
Sport of an earthquake, or a whirlwind-blast!
Where golden crosses, jewelled shrines and chalices
Mingle with wrecks of sumptuous royal palaces.

Rare alabaster, with embossed rich pyx,
From dainty lady's chamber sardonyx,
Enamel, and flushed porcelain immix:
Silk from far looms, with proud emblazonries,
Banner, and arras, glass of rainbow dyes,
Drums of great column, sculptured architrave,
Red dust of monarch from cathedral nave;
Ruby and sapphire, raiment sown with pearl,
Worn by fair scions of emperor and earl;
King's ancient crowns, and ermines, and tiaras,
Mid blocks from towers fallen on the wearers.
The Samson-strength of Peoples hath arisen,
Hurling to dust the palace and the prison:
Goaded to madness the blind giant bowed,
Till all the Commonwealth's huge pillars crashed
    with ruin loud!
Such chaos weltered when with furious cries
Mobs held blood-orgies in the Tuilleries!
But many a wilding bryony and bramble
Over the wilderness hath learned to ramble:
So grass, germander, violet, may vie
With malachite, or lapis lazuli,
In Rome, in Cæsar's palace, or grey baths
Of Caracalla; among sweet green paths,
Anemones and lilies fair enshrine
Red porphyries, or rich aventurine.

Melcha.

    Upon a crowning cornice crumbling grey
Stand two young lovers, beautiful as day.
Their lips meet, and their delicate limbs are twining;
Psyche and Erôs so were carven inclining.
There falls a sunset blush upon their whiteness,
While ever and anon a pulse of over-passionate brightness
Lightning-like thrills the rosy-flushing forms.
Opposite gazed a visage dark with storms,
All marred and riven, a crag tempest-worn;
Gazed with alternate joy, and grief, and scorn.
Like a fallen angel, it hath terrible beauty;
While fain to breathe an empyrean of Duty,
Its frame colossal, and sublimely moulded
Strains ever and anon from sloughs that hold it
Among these ruins, waving a wide pinion
Of snowy plume, that pants to have dominion;
Yet fails to free the angel altogether,
Who seems an eagle taunted by a tether—
A mire, alive with myriad coiling things,
Draining the life-blood, mocking the white wings!
Those swarthy limbs appear like lava, yet
Smouldering sullen: they were a fire-jet
From some volcano; ye, white wings of snow!
Love formed you of yonder Alp, that from below
Soars in high Heaven, with pure eve aglow.

'Tis as though ye were broken of a shaft,
Aimed by some cruel jealous god, who laughed,
Seeing how true it speeded : writhe, O man!
Presumptuous Titan, thou Promethean!

    Not far hence a pure Alp abides in light,
Gemmed with live sapphires, cloven with torrents,
    yonder
Girdled with forests : how he soars in might,
While ocean at his feet makes everlasting thunder!
Most wistfully the man contemplates Nature's glory;
And now the undying idyl of a lover's story;
Now with a bitter smile beholds an altar,
Betwixt him and the pair; Fate will not falter,
Offering youth, sweet sacrifice to Death!
The very twain, whose delicate arms enwreathe
Before him as alive, he sees low laid
Here, as on some revolt's red barricade
Young men and maidens, lately bold and hot,
With hoary sire and little child, lie shot;
So these have ceased from loving, and are not,
Lying fair-frozen in a mortal shade.
Their names are manifold; yet these may be,
Who loved in isles Ionian, Juan and Haidee.
While he who stands, a sunset-smitten tower,
Leaning aside now, reaching hands of power,
Is called Childe Harold; Manfred; Cain; the Giaour.

Melcha.

The limed, morass-entangled, floundering
    angel,
A devil, as some deem, hath his evangel!
He sinks, he rises, he hath freed one foot—
Reaching a hand to lift some Manlike Brute—
Which is it? maimed and stunted in its growth;
From sheer disuse its eyeballs blinded both!
Like some weird reptile's from Carinthian caves,
A human thrall in subterranean graves.
Rags flutter from a shagged and leathern frame:
Its food was blows, its daily wage was shame:
Famine mid mortal wrongs long kept it tame.
Shut from free light and air 'neath church and palace,
This human thing lay cramped of human malice,
Through dull, slow centuries, till it retrograded,
Toward brute brows and jowls, the manhood
    faded.
See! how it crawls from forth a rift amid the ruin,
Gnawing and burrowing! alas! this wrought the
    terrible undoing!

    Now from the fingers of his other hand
The form colossal filters a fine sand,
Which seems a dust of all in the wide world,
Immingled with red dust that hath been human:
And while in smoke all vanishes, lips curled
Appear to scoff: Behold! O man, and woman,
Your hopes, your longings into ruin hurled!

But some illustrious spirits may be seen,
Where that disaster of the creeds hath been.
Bouddha, Rousseau, bold Luther, with rude Knox,
Iena, with Könisberg unwandering eyes
Bend where huge moveless adamantine blocks
Rest undisturbed, though the fair fabric flies,
That hath been reared thereover, like a mist,
Before a blast from God's old Anarchist.
Even as on the Lebanonian plain
A man beholds foundations vast remain,
Whose every stone Cyclopean hath length
Of sixty feet, being measured ; ruin-fraught
Temples were raised upon them ; all the strength
Of Genii, by Solomon compelled,
Hath poised the ponderous platform that rebelled,
Thwarting man's power to found,
One with very ground !
So Tadmor's mighty stones were brought ;
So Duty, and Love abide, with Postulates of Thought.

Beside these souls illustrious are more,
Kneeling, or standing proud ; but all adore.
Divine Love, very Christ, they worship all,
Whether or no upon His Name they call.

Melcha.

Upon a cloud-car, vaporous alabaster,
Swift, though the rider longs to travel faster,
Stood one, ethereal-limbed like Ariel,
Whose spear, the sunbeam of Ithuriel,
Touched many a bulk of pompous purple pride,
That lay imposing, overswollen beside
His chariot-course; when lo! an infant's bubble,
Each bursting freed the burdened air from trouble.
His car was winged with plumes of sunny snow,
Edgeless and downy; but the front below,
Isled in deep azure, wore a soft dove-grey,
Heaved and recessed, with many a tender play
Of hyacinth or harebell; visionary changes,
As subtle-fancy'd amorous wind arranges;
While white rims of the rear, resolved to spray,
Evanish all in oceans of deep day.
One-half sun's rondure the cloud-chariot stole
From vision; half burned wheel-like; aureole,
Relieved on opaline, of slant slim ray,
Streamed up aloft behind the angel form,
Whose wild eyes ever yearned to where a storm
Of ominous thunder hath a rainbow arch,
Shining from falling showers before his march:
Surely he held them rain of human tears,
Falling from founts of human woes and fears.
In this fair Form, like Hopes, or Memories,
Cythna, Alastor, Laon, meet the lovers' eyes.

During long weary, dreary intervals
The spirit was compelled in his vast halls
To leave his bride alone, while he explored
Realms of a world wherein he was a lord.
Realms of lone terrors, of bewildering awe,
That fascinate adventuring souls, and draw,
As with lodestones, or glittering weird eyes
Of anaconda, one to snatch the prize,
The jewel Truth from clefts of the crag Danger,
Up sheer and giddy cliffs a solitary ranger:
On steep snow-walls, where a mere whispered breath
May rouse the slumbering avalanche of death;
In dark grim chasms where daylight never cheers,
Only the lammergeyer, or corven peers;
In wintry caverns roofed with frozen tears,
Where mystic murmuring chill waters flow,
Rivers that are the souls of realms unrolled below.
He plucks the glory of the edelweiss,
Planting his feet in perpendicular ice;
Upward he clambers with stern axe and pole:
What shall daunt the indomitable soul?
Clouds may beleaguer with bewildering error,
Torrents may thunder, cataracts of terror,
But he will mount, till on the proudest crest

Sun-crowned he stands, a conqueror confessed,
Or hurled to atoms in the abyss unbaffled he will rest.

Behold! he flounders in a forest foul,
Where balefire eyes from stealthy things that prowl
Glare on him, as he girds him unto war;
And though his love must yet abide afar
From him contending, yet her soul, a star,
Beams on him holy influence from yonder,
Nerving his own to quell the lion-thunder.
Yet there too in strange frondage, or lush blossom
Hide youths and maidens with soft limbs and bosom,
Who with Circean spells would lure among them
Pilgrims for revelry; sweet songs they sung them;
Yet if one rested there, a mad desire
Possessed him, a fierce marrow-feeding fire.

Or he must toil upon a salt-scurf plain,
Whose barren light beats on the burning brain:
A sullen sea sleeps bitter to the taste;
Gaunt skeletons are strewn upon a bitter herbless waste:
So forth must fare sweet Melcha's errant knight;
Nor free from stain shines out that armour white.

And she would travel with him to the strife;
But wars and wanderings would wither her young
 life.
Yet she may pray for him, yea, send her love
Hovering o'er him like a holy dove,
And he behold faint glimmers from her ark,
The while he welters, lost in waters dark.

  She strove to assimilate when he was gone
The food that he would have her feed upon;
Pondered his words, or would retrace some scene,
Where with him her companioned feet have been.
Alas! the more she strove, the more she knew
Abysms impassable betwixt them two!
Not even those shades relieved the loneliness,
That did upon her fainting spirit press.
She could discern no shadowy moving throng
Those vast interminable aisles among.
Shadowy twilight! a cold prison crypt!
Eternal silence! awful glooms that slept!
Death weighed upon her, as she cowered, and wept.
Ah! very faintly she beheld the splendours;
And hardly her bewildered memory renders
Account to her of what dim ways impart
Views of the grand creative forms of art.
So, unfamiliar with some ancient pile,
A wandering guest may lose himself, the while
He seeks his chamber in a twilit tangle

Melcha.

Of corridor, and banquet-hall, dim cloister, and
    quadrangle.
She heard some murmuring of cold blind springs
Under huge crags, haunted by condor wings,
Where pine, or cedar to the sheer steep clings,
Nor ever ray of sunlight falls
Between stupendous granite walls.

Then she recalled what her confessor spake,
Warning her of weird lords below the lake.
For eerie things, whose semblances she saw
Lately within the columns, thrust a claw,
Or a dead hand to seize her; so it seemed,
When for a moment a tall column gleamed;
Muffled friar from shadowy cowl
Glaring with unearthly scowl.
Yea, once she met with one who seemed her
    Knight,
Victorious returning from the fight;
She throws her in his arms, all happiness;
And lo! she peers in horrible eyes deadwhite;
The caverned bosom crumbles in her caress!

"Yet ah!" she sighed, "if he would only
    stay
Humbly with me in mine own earthly day!

Can I not lure him to abide in peace
In my forefather's land ? win him release
From this eternal proud disquietude ?
Lead him to rest beneath our holy rood ?
I fear, for all the glories that so gleam,
It is the unholy glamour of a dream ! . . .
Though some profound black possibility
Opens before me when my Knight is nigh—
I dare not sound it ! Madness yawns thereby ! . . .
How may I breathe here underneath the wave ?
Or I must fly, or lure him from the cave !"

  So now she strove with eloquent sobs to win
Her fairy lover from the halls of sin ;
For so she deemed them, weeping o'er the loss
Of her own homely sanctuary-cross—
" I cannot mock my glorious destiny,"
He answered, a fierce lightning in his eye ;
" No, not for love, nor comfort, nor a bride !
Wilt thou not share with me my throne, my pride ?"
Then he spake bitter words of foolish gall
Anent her faith ; the faith of a mere thrall,
He dared aver, till she herself felt anger,
And there arose a hybrid-born vain clangour
Betwixt their loves ; dull mist enveloped all.
A chilling feud arose from good and evil;

Melcha.

Love's limpid springs were poisoned by the devil.
" I deem that what thine incantation vaunts
May be but water, and long waterplants!
I fear thee! there be stains upon thine armour!
What realms hast haunted? art thou mine own
    charmer?
Hast thou not sinned? art thou the paragon
I lately set my faith upon? . . .
Nay, if vague rumour muttered of some sin,
Vile men malign us, and I hoped to win
Thee from the peril: thou wilt not be ruled!
Courting the wily foe, thou wilt be fooled!
Why leave me here in darkness over long,
In chase of some conundrum, or a song?
Why wage in ghostly realms a shadowy war,
Scorning the warm world for a phantom far?
I fear to lose my footing, and my goal!
Yea, thou hast robbed me of my rest, my soul!
While thy proud thoughts through all the world
    would roll! . . .
Thy gloomy pavements heave beneath my feet,
And all thy pillars rocking seem to meet! . . .
Why did I leave my native sphere above?
Thou wilt be lost too! fly with me, my love!
And thou shalt be no more a wandering wraith,
But our own stalwart champion of the faith!"

"Unworthy of this royal realm of mine!
I snatched you from the dust to make you mine.
I deemed the sacred fire within your spirit
Smouldered; mine eager, breathing love may stir it—
No queen! mere common clay, for all fair seeming!
Of toys, and dress, and dross for ever dreaming;
In highest Heaven longing for the sound
Of beasts of burden on the common ground,
At their monotonous unsoulful toil;
Drawing mere water, ploughing stubborn soil;
That hinds, or royal, or rich, or clothed in rags,
May gnaw roots, if their plodding never flags!
May only masks and mummeries delight you,
Though to full feasts of Reason I invite you?
Will you not let me couch your filmèd eyes?
For all your Atys' priests' insensate lies,
Trust me! God's day, when one is used thereto,
Strikes grander than mere spangles red and blue;
Or ghostly spawn of humours in sick blood!
Though all your sacred books pronounce them good,
And God's veracious ambient air profane——
Come forth, and all your juggling ghosts will wane!—
Come from your blinded dungeons!—or remain!"

Melcha.

"Shall I resign my soul, my life, my hope,
Among mere shadowy fancies here to grope
For ever? why calumniate my creed?
You wise ones know not all our bitter need!
See yon dim millions of human lives,
Swarming in labour's dun defilèd hives,
Stunned with base sounds, immersed in dingy
 crafts!
Dare not disdain the star, the flower that wafts
Our unimprisoned souls! a moment lifts
From reeking pestilent squalors, through what rifts
So-ever, to blue skies, and woodlands fair,
Fresh flowing water, and sweet liberal air!
Hail! soilèd flower, dim star among the smoke
O'er ruinous roofs! faint heaven-dawn that broke,
Luminous pearl above man's misery,
Mute for a moment now, where lewd huts lie,
Surprised to shame of their own shamelessness,
Deep degradation, and Hells' hopelessness,
By the young Angel, Morning!
 Lo! one wonders,
Wakes unaware, and sees God, while she ponders;
Ere yet long, thin, black throats of factories
Soil with brown breath yon virginal pure skies;
While, by the pearly river flowing fast,
She muses on a mole, with many a mast
Of wealth-gorged hulls from foreign lands around
 her:

Diseased, debauched, God's youthful Morning
    found her!
Wilt block these from the ray above their roof,
Or hold them from the Saviour flower aloof,
Till they have fathomed your astronomy,
Or learn to babble jargonous botany?
Jesus, and Mary, human wants have met!
Why will ye rob poor souls of their one amulet?
For me, my lot is low! I will fall prone,
With those dull worshippers thou dost disown!"

    He held her in his arms: he groaned: he fled.
But on the floors of Night she reeled, she stumbled,
    and fell dead.

    Arousing, Melcha slowly gazed around:
Grey forms gigantic stand, with ne'er a sound;
Every ghost, relieved against a column,
Hath one vast-moulded hand enclasping solemn
The other arm, whose hand the visage muffled.
Their heads are bowed, their rocky robes unruffled
Fall, like a mountain flank, with gorge profound
Grey riven: columns congregated here
Have thunderous amplitude: aloft they rear
To heights unknown, roofed over with dim fear,
Forming one vasty chamber of sphered gloom,
On whose faint heart there weighs a huge dark
    Tomb:

Melcha.

Hewn out of solid Night it seemed, in form
Resembling some sarcophagus enorm
Of Bull Osirian, disinterred by Nile
From dull oblivion of Time's ponderous pile.
As Melcha gazed, she felt One had been there,
To whom the world clings with sublime despair.
"If He be there still, all is doubt and doom ;
I deemed that He was risen from the tomb" . . .
Stay ! did she hear within the sepulchre
A sound ? . . . " Wilt thou arise, Deliverer ?"
. . . She hears her own loud heart; nought else
   astir.
'But I will ask these guardians," she said,
"If He indeed be risen from the dead !"
Then, in a whisper, daring scarce to frame
The syllables of that beloved Name,
" Tell me !" she murmured : " Is the Saviour risen ?"
. . . From yonder Forms, from hollows of the prison,
In weird unearthly tones, the sound "Arisen !"
Rolled in upon her soul . . . Ah ! how to gauge
The dark significance of such reply ?
Despair's own long-drawn wail of inarticulate agony!
Shall this the soul's deep yearning doubt assuage ?
Behold ! reverberations infinite
All the vast vaults and labyrinths affright
To conscious desolation, fatherless, profound,
Whom dull Oblivion's anodyne consoled with
   slumber sound !

Lulled on its dungeon floor, the world's Despair
Wakes with a wail! "Arisen! would He were!"

 And then it seemed as though, from all the
  goolm
Of never-ending hollows round the tomb,
A never-ending multitude of souls,
Inwardly weeping, cloaked in mournful stoles,
Moved from one point toward the silent grave
Of Him who came our ruined race to save.
Passing, each turned; all haggard; some in tears:
Everyone, moving silent, disappears,
A hopeless mourner, in the Darkness facing
That Night, whence he emerged with melancholy
  pacing.
But one who laughed in that dim hall
Ghastlier seemed to her than all!

 At length she moaned, with voice of one that
  dies:
"Innumerable throng
Of human generations manifold! how long?
For ever shall I see your hopeless eyes?
Ah! let me perish! Ah! for mine own skies!" . . .
Dreamfully she hears the swells
Of water-muffled peals of bells.

III.

And with this utterance of all her being,
The appearance-world thereunto swift agreeing
Melcha flies!
. . . Lo! now she lies
In sunny grass :
Her own dear lake-land! in a water-glass
Shadows of green herbage flowing,
Whose leaning blades quench one another
    glowing!
On snowy petal of a frail windflower
Golden anthers hint the hour
By tremulously shadowing;
Blue shadows to air-ruffled verges cling.
Here she buries her pale face,
Rendering ecstasy for grace,
Sensible of only this,
That spring woodlands are a bliss.
Now the birch from bronzy stems
Buds alternate emerald gems,
Whose leaflets glossy glistening
Fairy-fanned are listening
Unto mellow-throated elves,
Merrily sunning their small selves,
Where a flutter of a rain
Of slim branches moves a stain

On the delicate lady-skin,
Pinky silver shadowed thin.
How she hears the turtle coo,
And a soft call of cuckoo,
The lake-ripple lisping,
Bluely, blithely crisping;
Views yon delicate larch-clouds
Heaving like the masted shrouds,
Vivid green in azure sky,
Murmuring how tranquilly!
Cherry, and pink apple blossom
Hanging foam in air's blue bosom;
How she scents the woodland smell,
She remembereth so well;
Lying silent in a trance,
As in hours of old romance!
While already croziered fern
In the sun begins to burn,
Though dim morning rime impearl
Wings of mavis and of merle.
. . . But at length upon her mind
The hell she hath left behind
Glareth dimly from afar,
Like eclipse, or baleful star,
While she gradually remembers
How her soul hath been hell's embers!
    "I will humbly seek confession!

Melcha.

So relieve this dire oppression!"
Thinking thus, she took her way
To where above the placid bay
Stands her well-beloved chapel,
Near her home among the apple.
The lake lay yonder as before;
Yet she knew the land no more!
What hath come to wood and field?
No answer may her musing yield.
There the sanctuary appears:
. . . Doth it totter as with years?
Lo! the crucifix of wood
Shrined where it hath ever stood:
She is on her knees before it . . .
But what awful change comes o'er it?
The bleeding head bowed on the breast
Turns away from her request;
Turns from her who would be blest!
And she feels she cannot pray;
Cannot find what she shall say!

Then she enters grief-amazed
The rude chapel ruin-crazed;
Weathered beams and walls inclined
To and fro, as in a wind.
All her wild tale she reveals
To the priest, nor aught conceals.

He, much moved, and sore astonished,
His weird penitent admonished
She was wound in mortal sin;
And, would she salvation win,
Hardest penance must endure;
Make herself a holy nun;
Banish all which might allure
Memory of that evil one,
Who in guise of a white angel
Drew her from the pure evangel!
" For evermore thou shalt forsake
Those enchantments of the lake!"
This was not the aged priest,
Wont to serve her holy feast,
Before she fled away from earth;
And Melcha felt a very dearth
In her heart, when he so stern
Bade her love for ever turn
From all memory of him,
Yonder in the waters dim.
Yet she feared the fatal spell—
Christ and Heaven! Love and Hell!
" We may scorn not common ground:
God hath wisely fenced us round:
Within I bleed from a deep wound!" . . .

When she hath arrived at home,
A stranger maiden sees her come,

Melcha.

(How the aged house did lean!
Other was the garden scene:)
Who on Melcha's face and dress
Looks wide-eyed; while with no less
Marvel Melcha looks on hers.
She with the strange maid confers;
And, naming her own family,
Asks if sister, or her sire,
Be in the house, or near the byre?
The maid, with terror in her eye,
Replies: "'Tis near a century,
Since, as they tell me, one so named
Lived here—there is a portrait framed
In the old mansion, dim with age,
That often doth my mind engage,
Hanging in the parlour old;
A lady, of whom strange things are told—
How she eloped with our lake-fairy . . .
Like you the picture looks! ah! Holy Mary!"

Then Melcha in a mournful dream
Turned away from where the gleam
Of her old home promised rest
To the weary and distressed;
While the maiden scared and pale
Fled within to tell her tale.

And Melcha went with drooping face
To her mother's resting-place.

But she found not the old stone;
In its place a whiter one,
Commemorative of some other,
Not her well-belovèd mother!
And confusion o'er her grew,
When the dates thereon she knew.
While on a headstone sunk among
Grass and darnel growing long,
Where weather-stains and lichen gather,
She spells the name of her old father . . .
And now the dear name of her sister.
Alas! how often in fond hope she kissed her
Melcha lies in the warm sun,
Murmuring, " I must be a nun!"

So she made herself a nun;
And a high repute she won
Among pale devotees who fast,
Afflict their souls, and bodies cast
Scourged upon the midnight stone,
Supplicating, making moan,
Lacerated with remorse
For sin's dark tyrannic force.
Yet, alas,! the demon doubt
Was not utterly cast out.
Still her exorcisèd devil
Would return to hold his revel;

And where slept Love's own warm grace
Alas! now was a desolate place;
In that lone hollow of her heart
Fiery fangs of serpent dart;
Nor Heaven's mild and holy balm
Fills her wounded soul with calm.
Yet fellow-feeling with the poor,
Enslaved and sorrowful, half wrought a cure :
The world-wide mystery of Fate
Fell upon her with all its weight;
But gleams of Love, and Righteousness
Over the welter of distress
From unimaginable quarters
Looked here and there upon the waters,
Deep, wan waters of our sorrow,
Murmuring of dark to-morrow.
Yea, and kindly thought for all
Lifts from sorrow's lonely pall.

But they who reft of consolation live
Feel the sad impotence of penury,
When, longing some sweet cordial to give,
Helpless, and dumb, and void they hear the cry:
"A drop to cool our tongues in this flame's
    misery!"
As one awaking after night,
Blind with blaze of sudden light,

To chaos was her nature hurled,
Paralysed for either world,
Since her wild audacious flight.

   Now once more a gleam Elysian
Dawns upon her, a new vision,
Other than the sight of old,
Wondrous, wide, more manifold.
Then she cried, "How bitter, love!
Aching hollows where should be
Love, and His tranquillity!
Alas! my soul would climb above!
Yet if thou sink for need of me?
Did I well to fly away,
Leaving thee alone to stray
Ever further from sweet day?
In those awful wilds art lost?
O to clasp thee, tempest-tost!
Ah! my Lord! Ah! not for ever
From mine own thou wilt me sever:
Nay! my husband, thou shalt prove
A mightier arm, though mine remove! . . .
Two hearts tangled in Love's girdle golden!
Who dreams they shall not be holden?
I am faint: I seem to feel
Some new change, for woe or weal."
Then she wandered through the brake,

Melcha.

Till she came upon the lake:
How wistfully she gazed, and gazed
Where the auroral billow blazed!

Ah! what is the wild thrilling trouble
In the sun's blithe water-double? . . .
Behold, from forth the waters blue
Burst the spirit O'Donoghue!

He openeth wide longing arms—
Though where are now the earlier charms?
How she wavereth on the brink!
In mortal faint she seems to sink;
Yet looking on him, whispereth: "He is
  risen!"
Then, all transfigured, yields her to the prison
Of his embrace! but this her lover now
Shines radiant, as never he hath shone.
"Yea, He is risen—though I know not how!"
Answers the other . . . and the twain are gone
Under the sun-reverberant tide:
The fairy Knight hath won his bride!

THE AGNOSTIC.

A GIRL, who dared not say the Christian creed,
Tho' rich in kindly heart and valorous deed,
Sang me a simple hymn with reverent tone.
Later, before Beethoven's cloudy throne
Symphonic, I stood, rapt and marvelling;
And there a vision loomed on shadowy wing.

The Maiden fair in spirit I beheld,
Her eyes pure shrines of loftiest intent,
Indomitable endeavour, never quelled
By violent misfortune, nor repelled
By dull resistance of indifferent
Vicissitude, but ever buoyant; her
On a frail arch of slow dissolving ice,
I saw mid mountains robed in snowy fur,
All inaccessible, a precipice
At either end inexorably steep,
Banning approach; around her slender form
Unfathomable abysses of the deep,

O'er her involved embroilment of the storm,
Thundering cloud; methought she stooped anon
With cordial of her glance to yield support
Unto some faltering or fallen one
Upon life's painful perilous pass, full fraught
With fear, convoying from nowhere to nowhither;
So teach the later sages, and her mind,
Swayed by the mastering Magia breathing thither
From the Time-Spirit, so believes; or blind,
Or eagle-orbed, He rules the answering helm
Of man's opinion; but the mellow tones
Of her sweet anthem fill the frozen realm
With human longing; the unhearing stones
Prolong the strains within their hollow hearts
Unknowing; 'tis a hymn of piteous prayer
For help from Him Who of His Life imparts,
Some hold, to mortals; but the maiden there
So deems not; wherefore I feel wonderment.
Whether she sang, because the melody
Held soothing for her soul, or if she bent
Her loftier flight, sustaining some who fly
On lowlier pinion faint and falteringly
With infant cradlesong they love to hear,
I know not, but her mellow-toned appeal
Wanders an orphan through a world of fear,
Where none regards, nor can regard, nor feel
With mortal man, emitting a faint ray

Of conscious hope within the soulless gloom,
That feebly quavers but a little way,
For a brief while in the eternal tomb,
That is the fathomless and infinite
Mother of all. And still serene the smiles!

But how sustains her the eternal Night?
With what poor toys, with what illusive wiles?
There were some flowers in the ice-crevices
Some tiny flowers of dear seraphic blue,
And rifts in tempest; but are those, or these,
Sisters to them in deep cerulean hue,
Evanishing when born, howe'er they please,
Sustainers of her very light of life?
Or is she strong for her unequal strife
Through yonder gleams of gold upon the rock?
Nay, they are elf-gleams glimmering to mock!

But she adores twin visionary Stars,
That in the abysmal hollows wax and wane,
Strange progeny of elemental wars,
Ravening in chasms of the unsouled Inane!
Duty, and Love, fair sister, and bold brother,
To spring in very deed from such a Mother!
Yea, spiritual tides of boundless being
Are billowing in the soul, a moment fleeing
From naught to naught unfathomably still:
Ghost from the gloom the miracle of Will!

The Agnostic.   167

A lovely child played on the crystal bridge,
And she played with him, they loved one another;
Alas! he faded from the icy ridge,
Like some soft flower, his delicate fleeting brother;
He swooned into the unholy void, he perished!
While she with anguish wept the flower she cherished.

And yet methought that in the shrouding storm
I could distinguish some ethereal form,
As of a fair child often hovering nigh,
Albeit no vision met the maiden's eye.
Yet on the appealing waves of her sweet hymn
Toward her some breathing cohort seemed to swim.
Till unaware an ominous sharp sound
Foreboded wreck and ruin of the arc;
Startled she gazed into the dusk profound,
Then calmly-grave appeared to mark
Annihilation's face confronting her,
While in a moment with still overthrow
Vanished the fair arch, and his eager stir
Of life for ever—Nay! behold the glow
Of some divine celestial surprise
Dawns in the dewy darkness of her eyes,
While unsustained she falls; for lo! the cold
Unfathomable hollow-hearted gloom
Grew warm hearts throbbing with a love untold;

The iron crags, built round her like a tomb,
Arms wound to ward with full-assured embrace;
Confused cloud-chaos, vasty vans that brood
Expansive o'er the darkness, with a grace
Of hallowing benediction for the rude
Sullen death-realm, unfounded and unformed,
Rousing a life within the grey womb, warmed
From their abounding! O grand countenance
Of guardian angels! once a drear expanse,
High snows aloof, indifferent! ye stars,
Luminous eyes, who gaze through pearly bars
Unslumbering! . . . A childish form floats hither,
The same who seemed before her eyes to wither;
She only lost him for a little while;
They greet again with still celestial smile.
For righteous Love, tho' visionless she be,
Buoys high the Soul o'er death's catastrophe,
Bears her triumphant on the central tide
Of universal Life, the immortal Bride.

THE DEATH OF LIVINGSTONE.

I.

"No mortal power shall turn me: I arise,
And will go forward, with my face for ever
Toward those fountains of the sacred river,
River still guarding from all mortal eyes
The hoary mystery of mysteries."
So vowed the pilgrim, chief of a strong band,
Who toil to wrest from Death the twilight land.
A deep resolve, more grand than midnight skies,
Glowed in his countenance; but face and form
Were marred and writhen with the lifelong storm.
While life's dark winter snowed upon his heart,
All wrathful elements howled forth, Depart!
Heaven with remorseless frown above him bowed;
Earth rose in whelming floods to help the cloud.

II.

Whelmed in the wild and terrible morass,
He wades, he swims, he flounders; he is borne

Upon the shoulders of dark men forlorn,
To whom the grandeurs of his spirit pass
By glorious contagion ; a foul mass
Of foes malignant o'er the man outworn
Clamour; disease his vitals doth harass,
Draining the life-blood ; mortal pain hath torn :
Until his faithfuls weave him a soft bed
Of boughs, and bear him among flowering reeds
And lotus-paven waters : overhead,
Languid from anguish, he in dreaming heeds
An eagle at dawn, whose ghostly voice is hurled,
As though he called one from another world.

III.

A world of waters—sounds of solemn sea,
As wind soughs wandering in rushes now :
But they have built with grass and limber bough
A hut for him who fainteth mortally.
"Lord, let not Hell prevail! be with me Thou!
May I sustain the load allotted me ;
And ere in England falls the winter snow,
May I be there, at home, with Victory! . . .
. . . Deep is the desolation of my soul :
It may be I am failing ere my task
Full-ended : in my wake no champion
Of light is following ; where waters roll

The Death of Livingstone.

On fair Nyassa, Death's dark navies bask!
Mary lies in her forest grave alone!

IV.

"Alone her face, and one more, dear as hers,
Avail red haunting horrors to dispel.
O my dark race, plunged in the abyss of Hell!
Sweet babes and women, beneath slow murderers!
Tortured I start from slumber—weeping blurs
Mine eyes for memories no words may tell.
. . . Ere the young linnet in a soft nest stirs,
I would be home, my work accomplished well!"
. . . Drearily day faints, moaning into night;
The dark men sadly lose their fading sight,
Cowering silent by the watchfire light.
Beasts growl in jungles of Ilala land;
Far nightbirds wail on Lulimala strand;
Trees fire-illumined murmur, a tall band.

V.

"Is it our people who are shouting so?"
The dark and tender follower replies,
"A buffalo from far corn-fields with cries
Men scare." . . . The spirit wanders to and fro,
Like some dim waters' aimless ebb and flow;
'Is this the Luapula?'" . . . whose surmise

Gently the man dissolves: then in a low
Alien tongue, and with faint, filming eyes,
The weary wanderer wistfully inquires,
" How far is Luapula ?" falling soon
To slumber. . . . Later, after night's chill noon,
His boy-attendant, running toward the fires
Out of the hut, where both were sleeping, said,
"Come to the Master! for I am afraid."

VI.

They, rising, hasten to the cabin door;
Where, by a feeble taper, which adheres
To a worn wooden travelling-case, appears
The form of one who kneels upon the floor,
The head bowed in the hands enclasped before
The body. Reverent they pause: none hears
A sound of breathing; louder than of yore
The low watch-pulse affronts foreboding ears.
At length one, timid, touches the grey head.
Stone-cold, and silent! Livingstone is dead!
Lifting his arms to God above the crowd
Of trampling furies, broken, but not bowed,
His mighty soul went out: the slave in chains
Moans: the ghost-eagle calls: Hell laughs: Night
    reigns!

VII.

The cold hands call upon abysmal Gloom :
Strange frondage murmurs in a darkling morn :
Orphaned men cower round the fires forlorn :
Nile shrouds his fountains : the dim living tomb
Of Africa still closed, Death's blank-eyed doom,—
No face beloved, no land where he was born,—
Guerdons the warrior! No prayed-for bloom
Of home-love crowns him ere the year outworn ;
But while faint eyes look far away with trust,
Death spurns the soul's quenched altar in the dust !
. . . Is all, then, failure ? Lives no Father there ?
Do living hearts but supplicate dead air ?
Is this the end of the Promethean
Indomitable, all-enduring Man ?

VIII.

Who calls it failure ?
                    God fulfils the prayer :
He is at home ; he rests ; the work is done.
He hath not failed, who fails like Livingstone !
Radiant diadems all conquerors wear
Pale before his magnificent despair ;
And whatsoever kingdoms men have won,
He triumphs dead, defeated, and alone,

Who learned sublimely to endure and dare!
For holy labour is the very end,
Duty man's crown, and his eternal friend;
Reason from Chaos wards the world's grand whole;
All Nature hath Love's martyrdom for goal.
Who nobly toils, though none be nigh to see,
He only lives,—he lives eternally.

IX.

Night melts in glory; royal-robèd Sun
Glowingly deepens, like a martial blare,
Awakening mountain, lake, and forest fair;
Assumes all Africa for royal throne.
Slaves, to the height of their great master grown,
With souls unfettered, and free limbs, prepare
The wondrous march, whose Europe-shaming care
Made all his faithful fortitude our own,
Enshrined for men the man magnanimous,
A beacon for all races and for us!
Yet if no rumour had survived the grave,
If all were whelmed in dark Ilala-wave,
Yon very woods and waters in their dim
Hearts would have lost no memory of him!
They, in their mystic message to all time,
And all the worlds, have thrilled with the sublime
Story of man; God reassumes the life;
He crowns unseen the labour and the strife.

The Death of Livingstone.

Labour is full fruition in the bud,
And faith, possession dimly understood.

Mortal defeat blows oft the clarion
Of resurrection o'er an indolent world
Death-dreaming, louder than hath e'er been blown
From visible triumph ; the freed soul unfurled
A conquering flame, arousing the dull plain
Of common souls to kindle in his train,
Heroic-moulded, woke the silent dust
To songful flowers of helpful love and trust;
Inspired the world's dead heart to throb victoriously;
So they awake to life, who warring desperate die!
Yea, in the smile of some Divine deep Peace,
Our faithful find from storms of earth release.

BYRON'S GRAVE.[7]

NAY! Byron, nay! not under where we tread,
Dumb weight of stone, lies thine imperial head!
Into no vault lethargic, dark and dank,
The splendid strength of thy swift spirit sank:
No narrow church in precincts cold and grey
Confines the plume, that loved to breast the day:
Thy self-consuming, scathing heart of flame
Was quenched to feed no silent coffin's shame!
A fierce, glad fire in buoyant hearts art thou,
A radiance in auroral spirits now;
A stormy wind, an ever-sounding ocean,
A life, a power, a never-wearying motion!
Or deadly gloom, or terrible despair,
An earthquake mockery of strong Creeds that were
Assured possessions of calm earth and sky,
Where doom-distraught pale souls took sanctuary,
As in strong temples. The same blocks shall build,
Iconoclast! the edifice you spilled,
More durable, more fair: O scourge of God,

Byron's Grave.

It was Himself who urged thee on thy road;
And thou, Don Juan, Harold, Manfred, Cain,
Song-crowned within the world's young heart shalt
    reign!
Whene'er we hear embroiled lashed ocean roar,
Or thunder echoing among heights all hoar,
Brother! thy mighty measure heightens theirs,
While Freedom on her rent red banner bears
The deathless names of many a victory won,
Inspired by thy death-shattering clarion!
In Love's immortal firmament are set
Twin stars of Romeo and Juliet,
And their companions young eyes discover
In Cycladean Haidee with her lover.

    May all the devastating force be spent?
Or all thy godlike energies lie shent?
Nay! thou art founded in the strength Divine:
The Soul's immense eternity is thine!
Profound Beneficence absorbs thy power,
While Ages tend the long-maturing flower:
Our Sun himself, one tempest of wild flame,
For source of joy, and very life men claim
In mellowing corn, in bird, and bloom of spring,
In leaping lambs, and lovers dallying.
Byron! the whirlwinds rended not in vain;
Aloof behold they nourish and sustain!
In the far end we shall account them gain.

SNOWDROPS.

O DARLING spirits of the snow,
   Who hide within your heart the green,
How e'er the wintry wind may blow,
   The secret of the summer sheen
      Ye smile to know!

By frozen rills, in woods and mead,
   A mild pure sisterhood ye grow,
Who bend the meek and quiet head,
   And are a token from below
      From our dear dead,

As in their turf ye softly shine
   Of innocent white lives they lead,
With healing influence Divine
   For souls who on their memory feed,
      World-worn like mine.

NOCTURNE.

The shadowy portals of dim death
Unfold alluringly,
And all my soul importuneth
Unfathomed worlds for thee !
O ye illimitable realms
Of awful amplitude,
From your immensity that whelms
I crave one only good !
From unimaginable wealth
My soul demands but this,
Nor fame, nor power, nor gold, nor health,
A little child's warm kiss !
If I may feel him when I part,
And if he greets me then,
Unsorrowing will my weary heart
Forsake the haunts of men.
Ah me ! engulphed in the wild storm,
That drifts the lost like leaves,

Nocturne.

Mine arms may never clasp thy form,
Where a still water heaves,
Where God's own sunlight cleaves to thee,
My holy little child!
Yet through a storm-rent might I see
Thy joy, my undefiled,
I deem that I could bear my fate,
However dark and drear;
But I behold no Heaven's gate
From our confusion here!
I think the love between us twain
May raise me for awhile;
Yet if the shadow of my pain
Would only cloud thy smile,
Ah! move not near me, till my doom
Of whirlwind, ice, and fire
Be all accomplished in the gloom,
And I be lifted higher!
Our Love shall save, whate'er delays,
And thou be fain of all thy dole!
Dear Love hath many secret ways,
Whereby She steals from soul to soul;
Are any hells beyond the rays
Of Her all-healing miracle?
If the Abysses could devour
Thy love and mine, then all were lost:

But where Love breathes, a fadeless flower
May bloom from Death's inveterate frost !
And though the fiends would whelm me low
With mine own sins for ponderous stones,
Child-angels all around me flow ;
I loved them ; they have heard my moans !

BEETHOVEN.[3]

The mage of music, deaf to outward sound,
Rehearsing mighty harmonies within,
Waved his light wand; the full aerial tides
Ebbed billowing to rear of him, o'erwhelmed
All listening auditors, engulphed, and swept
Upon the indomitable, imperial surge
To alien realms, and halls of ancient awe,
Which are the presence-chambers of dim Death:
The grand departed haunt this mountain-sound!
Cliffs, and ravines, and torrent-shadowing pines,
A pomp of winds, and waters, and wild cloud
The enchanter raises: then the solemn scene
Evanishing, lo! delicate soft calm
Of vernal airs, young leaflets, and blithe birds,
The cuckoo and the nightingale, with bloom
Of myriad flowers, and rills, and water-falls,
Or sunlit rains that twinkle through the leaves,
And odorous ruffled whirlpools of the rose.
Anon, some wondrous petal of a flower,

An ample velvet petal, slides along
A luminous air of summer, visibly
Mantling a vermeil glory in the blue;
And now thin ice films clearest water; now
Our youngest angel whispers out of heaven,
And all the choir of his companions
Let loose their rapture on swift sudden wings,
Sunshine released unhoped-for from a cloud!
Slant rays of opal through the clerestory;
Dawn over solemn heights of lonely snow,
Aerial dawn, that deepens into day;
A congregating of white seraph throngs,
Who hold the realms of ether with white plume,
And with a sweet compulsion lift to heaven!
Ye, Harmonies, expand immeasurably
The temple of our soul, and yet are more,
Than earth can bear; within the courts above
Ye may expatiate majestical,
Native, at home! poor mortals hide their tears,
With caught breath, nor may follow: mountain stairs,
Platform on platform, ye aspire to God!
His infinite Soul who bore you is immortal,
And ours, in whom reverberates your appeal!
O music-marvel! how your royal river
Mirrors our life; there breathes exhaled from it
Sorrow and joy, and triumph and despair;

Beethoven.

Your eagle flight is through the infinite,
No barriers to prison from the immense.
Yours the large language of the heights of
    Heaven!
Now lonely prows, exploring realms unknown,
Unpiloted, beneath wan alien stars,
Your strain recalleth, keels of lonely thought,
Wandering in some sublime bewilderment,
To pioneer where all the world will go,
Now merry buoyancy, as of a boat,
That dips in billowy foam at morning tide.
Ye are alive with yearnings of young love,
Or sombre with immeasurable woe,
Sombre with all the terror of the world,
Wild with the awe and horror of the world,
Begloomed like seas empurpled under cloud,
Reeling and dark with horror of the wind,
Or pale, long heaving under a veiled moon.

Then, with the fading symphony, the master
Drooped, earthward fallen through mortal weariness,
From heights empyreal; he faced the slaves
Now silent, with stilled instruments, who wrought
A fabric for his high imagination,
A chambered palace-pile of echoing sound,
A shadowy fane within the realms of sense.
Drear Silence seems to him to reign; when lo!

A touch, at which he turns! the audience,
Vast, thronged, innumerous have risen before him!
Unhearing the loud storm of their applause,
He sees the tumult of their ocean joy
Thunderously jubilant, in eloquent eyes,
And flashing gems, waved kerchiefs, and moved feet!
So then the solitary master feels
The heart-clasp of our infinite human world,
And bows rejoicing not to be alone.

  Ah! brothers, let us work our work, for love
Of what the God in us prevails to do!
And if, when all is done, the unanswering void
And silence weigh upon our souls, remember
The music of a lonely heart may help
How many lonely hearts unknown to him!
The seeming void and silence are aware
With audience august, invisible,
Who yield thank-offering, encouragement,
And strong co-operation; the dim deep
Is awful with the God in Whom we move,
Who moulds to consummation where we fail,
And saith, "Well done!" to every faithful deed,
Who in Himself will full accomplish all.

NORTHERN SPRING.

MEADOW and woodland
Dwindle away,
Delicate azure in
Delicate day,
An infinite ocean of
Wave-like woods;
Old elms remember
Earlier moods,
A young leaf-rapture
On their gnarled boughs;
Thorns sing a carol of
Soft May-snows;
The young laburnum
Overwells,
With peals of bloom from
Inaudible bells;
Sweet peals of laughter of
Noiseless gold
His leafy bowers
Delight to hold!

A crimson May-foam
Flushes fair,
Soft yellow falls in a
Blithe blue air.
Daisies and kingcups!
Children's flowers!
They wander, and pull them,
Hours on hours;
A childish laughter
Delights the day,
Sweet heavens are happier,
While they play;
Golden boats of the
Kingcups float,
The voice of the cuckoo is
Heard remote,
With voice of the turtle,
Sounds so mild,
They breathe of the spring-time,
Earth's young child;
They breathe of the Peace at the
Heart of things,
Who hath taken the wide world
Under Her wings.
They tell of my boyhood,
They tell of my boy,
They tell of him folded

Northern Spring.

Beyond annoy;
The groves are a cloudland
Of glowing green,
With borders embosomed in
Warmer sheen.

I who longed for the whispering cool of the grove
Stole to the valley of verdurous gloom,
Where a nightingale sings evermore to his love,
As though man knew no sorrow, nor earth e'er a tomb.
A bird hath a nest in a twilight of leaves,
All woven of mosses, and lichen and down;
An eye there is glistening, a bosom there heaves;
You may see there love's miracle, when she hath flown—
Four delicate ovals, flecked faintly with wine—
She is guarding the mystical marvel of life,
The wind-flower illumines her bowery shrine,
And the pale flame of primrose around her is rife.
But the nightingale sings! how he sings! what a song!
Clear water that falls, or meanders in day;
From a smooth stem of sound, that is mellow and long,
Notes of fountainous blossom are lavished in play;

And one of his delicate silvery measures
Recalls one who whips a clear watery glass ;
My springs and my summers, aerial pleasures,
A fair haze, while I hearken, how fleetingly pass !
And O what a soft-pleached musical woof
The innumerous melody weaveth in air !
More subtle and rich than the verdurous roof
Of foliage marrying over me fair.
Ye enwind with your music, enmeshed, flushed with bloom !
I am sheathed, like a chrysalid silken, with joy ;
I forget that the world hath a grief or a gloom,
Ye scatter your songs on the grave of my boy.
Ah ! where are the conflict, the care and the pain,
The cruelty, feebleness, folly, or sin ?
O Philomel ! pour your melodious rain !
Open your Paradise ! welcome me in !
O lark, wild with ecstasy ! lost in the light,
We are ever afar from your shadowless land !
Our Philomel, she is more near to our night,
More nigh to her gloaming of green we stand.
For while her song-pulses may vie with the stars,
We have known in the clear, limpid airs of the South,
She hath one long low burden akin to our tears,
Wherein joy lieth hid for renewal of youth,
Deliciously low, like a plaining flute,
Or water in moonlight, of silent foot.

Philomel is a child of the daylight and dark;
Where the willow-leaf bathes in the flame of the
  moon,
She sings; all the night listens; not to the lark
Will a sorrowful heart of men turn for a tune!
And I think that the world, if it hold such a glad-
  ness,
Must be sound to the core, whatsoever befall:
Our birds, for all wrong, sorrow, wildering madness,
Do but echo young hearts in the heaven, who
  know all!

THE TWO MAGDALENES.[9]

Art thou indeed repentant? though thy look
Be concentrated on the holy book?
Thy glowing wave of bosom makes it warm!
Thine oval face-flower leaneth on an arm
Luxuriantly moulded, negligent.
A Mediterranean-blue robe hath lent
Disclosure to the undulating form,
Reclining languid in a shadowy place
Mid murmuring leaves, and there thy mellow grace
The Sun divines, who, passing through the grove,
Illumines throat, and bosom with still love.
Art thou indeed repentant? all thy youth
Mantling within thee! doth the perfect mouth
Weary of kissing? Here 'tis cool and fresh
For musing on the frailty of the flesh,
For shadowy contemplation, and sweet sorrow!
But who may prophesy of thy to-morrow?
The seven devils in thee, did they go?

The Two Magdalenes.

Or do they only sleep that they may grow?
Smouldering slumberous in thine almond white,
They may awake with renovated might!
Thou, blessing the brown earth with bare light foot!
I think they only parted to recruit.
When the world leaves you, worn with use, ye turn;
Nay, rule the world-illusion while ye burn!

A later painter showed her otherwise.
Under the domination of deep eyes,
She knows no more these lovers, for the wings
Of lovelier life new-born in her; she flings
The jewels from her, for the Pearl He brings.
In presence of her Lord, no fair and sweet
She knoweth, save to lay them at His feet.
Our splendid world dies, very dull and dim;
The woman in her seeth only Him!

WINTER.

I.

BLUE-GREEN firs waver in a water wan,
Save where red bole, fir-robe unmoved, and dim
Show the keen wizard Frost prevails upon
Even rivers; a low clink bewrays a slim
Bird, who hath lighted on the marge to drink.
Aerial webs invisible, that link
Sere, russet fern with glume of yellow grass,
And green fir-needle, are palpable star-chains
Of fairy jewel; from furze-point they pass;
Every thin, green lance of broom sustains
Like burden; all are fledged with crystal soft,
Mist frozen in plumelets; many a taper tuft
Adorns the wine-stained bramble, and the blade,
Or bronzy twigs of trees bereft of shade.

II.

Heath white with frost, and orange reeds are fair,
Beneath yon sombre masses of cold firs,

Winter.

Wave-mirrored, while a silver birch's hair
Hangs, like dark smoke, athwart the leaden air.
Winter upon small marish pools confers,
As on our panes, with palms and wreaths of hers,
A delicate starflower beauty, rivalling
All fragile water-petals of sweet spring :
Adorns wine-dark, ferruginous fens and ling,
Desolate lowlands where the bittern booms.
And now at nightfall, from where forest looms,
A dragon train wails 'thwart the solitude
Flame-breathing, with a long self-luminous brood,
And livid, long low steam among grey glooms.

III.

Snow falls, hath fallen, all the land is white.
Pure snow clings frozen to labyrinths of trees :
They, in the narrow lane, aloft unite ;
Winter hath clothed with a pure foliage these,
Pitying them, bereft of spring's delight.
How fairylike their veiled pale silences!
Feathery phantoms a grey mist informing
With beauty, as frail corallines dim sea.
Some alien planet our earth seems to be!
Earth lies fair in her shroud and slumbereth;
So fair the pure white silence of dim death!
Lo! the sun's fleeting phantom faintly warming

Mists into heaven-blue, while they flush and flee :
Budding birchsprays hang laughing jewelry
Of opal ice athwart the lift that clears ;
Clinking it falls, or melts in jubilant tears.

IV.

Gaily snow flounceth earthward in the sun,
Or frozen glistereth with icy edge
To windward of the elmbole ; birds in dun
Plumage, fair-formed elves, whistle in the hedge,
Scatter its ermine mantle ; as they run,
Dint earth's blithe stainless carpet ; shake the foam
Splashed upon all green brambles, and red-fruited
Hollies, or thorns, or briars, where they roam ;
Our ever sweet-songed robin richly suited,
And birds reserving for a leafier home,
And lovelier lands the voice wherein love luted,
Erewhile in yon dead summer: shadows blue
Nestle where beast, or man hath trodden deep
In crisp, starred snow ; fur mantles fair endue
Thatched roof, wain, barn and byre, while they creep
To a fringe of diamond icicle ; the waters are asleep.
No skaters whirr and whirl, as erst, upon the imprisoned grey

Winter.

Plain of the river; rosy children sliding, shout
    and play:
Pile the illumining logs within, and let them
    crackle gay!
Bright holly and green mistletoe cheering our
    hearths we keep :
Warm glint the polished chairs and glasses, while
    yule-fires glow deep.
But when dear babes lie dreaming, with a halo near
    the moon,
And at their nursery doors are left small fairy-
    appealing shoon,
There will float a voice of mystic bells over earth's
    pale swound,
And sweet sad fays of memory to haunt us in their
    sound!

1874.

IN ITALY.

By the low light of the moon, love,
By the low light of the moon,
From her enchanted swoon, love,
The cypress woke and sighed,
Beyond a wooded mountain, the sea that hath
    no tide
Murmured to the moon.

The wilding passion-flower, love,
The wilding passion-flower,
Dishevelled in her bower, love,
Whispered dewy-eyed,
And thou near vine-immantled column by my
    side
Whisperest, my flower!

SONNETS.

POLITICAL SONNETS.[10]

I.

GREAT-HEARTED statesman, eagle-eyed, and pure!
Our folly, weary, as in days of old,
With one monotonously just, grew bold
To cast thy virtue from them! We endure,
Whose honour once was like the Pole secure,
A shameless reign of brazen-faced Untruth,
Fair with false hues, the mortal foe to ruth,
And equal right. What golden salve may cure
These inward wounds? Our fiery standards wave
Over more ravaged lands; ah, Liberty!
Once, where they dawned auroral, all thy brave
Sons rallied round triumphant; now, the dye
Upon them is thy heart's blood—to the grave
'Tis England thrusts thee, with cold mockery!

II.

Barren the conquest of rich, populous lands,
When the proud conqueror, foredoomed and blind,

Himself the very ground hath undermined
Beneath his legions. Wheresoe'er he stands,
Earth reels from his unfaith; brute force commands
Now but fierce fear, even where men's hearts inclined
Lately to cherish his right rule, with bands
Of sober use, and feeling intertwined,
Light-bound for mutual service, lord and thrall.
O ye stern rocks of either continent,
Where we do murderous battle! will ye fall,
And hide from the Lamb's vengeance? We were sent
To bless the Lord's own little ones; we went
To roll in blood and flame their homes, and all!

III.

England, a tyrant! Spirits, who have fought
For Progress on the bloodless battle-fields,
Where generous Reason's mild persuasion wields
A mightier arm than ever anvil wrought!
Ye, who with life man's heritage have bought
Upon the block, the stake, the deadly plain,
Your Human Fabric, built with souls, to nought
Falls, by the ruining hands of men profane!
England, who led the vanguard of God's host,
And heralded His rule to the blind world,

Weak, alien races, robber-like, hath hurled
Earthward, and grinds with armèd heel! 'Tis lost,
The Holy Cause, through Her black treacheries—
Freedom's great Temple-pillar prostrate lies.

IV.

Lost for a while! Nay, we repent! We would
Cease from inhuman insolence and crime,
And God's high name profaned, the while we climb
Stairs of grim Power, and Greed, defiled with blood,
To lay before their shrine foul idol-food
Of human welfare murdered. We dare name
The God who hath abased Himself to shame,
And want, and death, for Love, upon the Rood,
Sue for Christ's blessing, while we crucify
His poor, who are the apple of His eye!
Now, England sober, to herself returned
From orgies of deep, drugged bewilderment,
Invokes thee, righteous patriot, whom she spurned.
Come forth, our hope, Achilles! from thy tent!

THE CATHEDRAL.

Cathedral heights among the midnight stars,
Ye are as mountains in sublimity!
Your phantom towers, aerial forms on high,
By whispering groves surrounded, for our wars,
And puny whirl of foolish strife, that mars
Our poor brief lives, arraign humanity;
The vasty fane through rifts of shadowy tree
Some city of departed souls appears.
But in the morning, solemn sounds are rolled
Through forest gloom of jewelled nave and aisle;
Young tones swift-soaring mazy flowers unfold,
Now fall like dew, now float like a sun-smile;
The sweet wind of their music seems to mould
Yon high fan-roof that undulates the while.

Ely, 1884.

VERY DEATH.

THERE are worse deaths than Death, for Love may die,
And Hope, and Joy, and holy Innocency,
With Faith ; yea, all we have leaned upon may fly,
May fail, may change ; no longer beautiful,
A very spirit fade to dark and dull,
Withering toward dissolution ; firm-knit mind
Weltering in confusion, we may find
The large brain narrow, the warm heart unkind ;
And there may come an hour when we shall bow
Our heads for him, whom we have mourned till now,
Thanking the Powers that they resumed his breath,
While he was yet a child, unknowing Death,
The very death ; ourselves, who are left alone,
Praying that we may die, and turn to stone.

MADNESS.

She spake of madness, telling that the worst,
As found incurable, was when men deemed
The world all happy, when misfortune seemed
Supreme good fortune, and the lot accurst
Appeared true bliss; what lowered repulsive erst
Was changed to lovely, all-delightful gleamed,
Evil a cloud into blue heaven dispersed:
Beyond hope these illusions are esteemed.
'Twas spoken in good faith, unheedingly;
Yet they perchance the inner truth divine,
And if we hope to heal, the madmen we!
I would such hallowed lunacy were mine,
Here, where some say 'tis better not to be!
What fool would cavil o'er this anodyne?

THE SANCTUARY.

A PASTORAL scene! a region of deep peace,
Where Nature and the Home dwell hand in hand
Harmonious; one finds a sweet release
Here from all evil and the world; the land
Heaves undulating mildly, and the elms
Lift murmuring boughs umbrageous in blue air.
There is a river moving in the realms
Of meadow, fallowland, and harvest fair;
A velvet lawn slopes downward from the home,
Illumed with flowers, to meet with a churchyard,
That seems a sister; unaware we roam
Athwart the rill's division thitherward,
Nor feel a difference; for meek mild flowers
On velvet turf love either; the dear graves
Have headstone, or white cross; the quiet hours
Are told, as if in dream, to the green waves,
That heave above the sleepers, and soft winds
Around the church-tower, by the voice therein.
Yon hamlet nested in his orchard finds

The sunny pastor hath large heart akin
To humble joy and sorrow ; where he dwells
Abideth a warm halcyon atmosphere
Of hallowed calm, as in lone summer dells.
Within the house, and in the landscape here,
All is serenely soothing ; the grave words,
With looks, and deeds, arise from a deep spring
Of faith perennial beneath the sense,
No earthly heats may doom to perishing,
Because the birth of it is not from hence,
But in the heart of the eternal hills,
Pure child of ocean and eternal sun,
No fleeting wealth from casual-flowing rills,
Cool and refreshing when the rest are gone.

  In yonder church the same pervading calm,
For troubled souls world-weary very balm !
Here is a sacring of pure lives and prayers,
Of holy aspirations, and kind cares ;
For here the brethren of the Holy Ghost
Worshipped and pondered, battled with the host
Infernal; here, in early morning, while
White wings of cloud, enjoying the sun-smile,
Pass by the mullioned window-lights in blue,
Soft seven-fold flame of tapers will imbue
With warm translucency the white wax end
Of either ; seven-fold flame will upward tend

The Sanctuary.

From candles culminant on either side
A brazen candelabrum branching wide,
Over an altar, in a deep twilight
Of cloth of gold, with broidery bedight,
Whereon are chalices for holy wine,
And crucifix of gold, the mystic sign.
There stands the priest white-robed, and whispers low,
While men and women reverent below
Kneel to receive the emblems; there is lent
Reposeful calm from yonder monument,
Where the recumbent forms absorbed in prayer
Ever abide in shadowy cool air;
They take no heed of our deluding time,
Our dewy eve, midnoon, or morning prime;
They, tranced to marble, ever rest in peace,
So that we long to be with them and cease.
And here awhile our weary sails are furled,
Here in a haven folded from the world;
Here we may taste awhile the bread of life,
And breathe an atmosphere aloof from strife;
A ray of comfort steals into our prison
From happy souls, who with the Lord are risen.

NOTES.

GENERAL NOTE.

THE author, even where he speaks in his own person, hopes not to be held responsible for all the negations he may have expressed or implied in poems ranging, as regards their date of composition, over several years, a few of them having been written some time before his " Little Child's Monument," published in 1881. The earlier poems, however, have been revised; but, save in one instance, only the form of them, not the substance, has been altered. Yet, where not impersonal, all remain as expression of temporary moods, feelings, or ideas.

His thanks are due to Messrs. Chatto and Windus, Messrs. Isbister, and the proprietors of the *Contemporary Review*, for permission to republish poems printed in the *Contemporary*, *Gentleman's Magazine*, and *Good Words*.

NOTE 1, *page* 15.

I am indebted for this incident to a writer in the *Daily Telegraph*.

NOTE 2, *page* 20.

See " Underground Russia," Stepniak, p. 208.
A young man, the better to guard the secret of the revolutionary printing-press, thus effaced himself from all record and recognition among the living, dwelling in a poisoned atmosphere, without ever leaving it, until, the place being discovered and captured by the police, he committed suicide.

NOTE 3, *page* 44.

Suggested by the fire in the Ring Theatre, at Vienna, after which to the poor, as chief mourners, was allotted the post of honour at the funeral in St. Stephen's.

NOTE 4, *page* 60.

See Pliny.

NOTE 5, *page* 81.

The metres of *Suspiria* and *Thalatta* were suggested to me by the sound of the sea ; that of *Suspiria* is of course a modification of the hexameter, with rhyme in the alternate lines. To my ear it appears that the hexameter ought not to be written with two single words in the last (trochaic) foot, but that in this particular, at least, the structure of the verse in its native sources should be respected.

NOTE 6, *page* 106.

This poem is suggested by old Killarney legends. But though it is to be read primarily as a fairy-tale, it is also intended to convey a further meaning. Only that is not to be sought in every detail, because I think that in all works of art, the story, form, or concrete presentment of whatever kind, ought to be paramount, and the inner significance only implicit, or suggested. The reader or spectator, moreover, has cause for complaint if the artist should, by over-insistence on this latter element, foreclose the right of all to find their own lesson or significance in a work of art. Barely didactic art there cannot be. But there should be more in a poem of this kind than the maker ever put there. Whether I have here succeeded in doing what I wished is of course another question. Time and Place are not respected in the world of enchantment, which is also that of Thought, whence all Creation issues. And Melcha, once having lived there, can no longer find the same old home-world, to which she was accustomed, when she would fain do so, the quiet, innocent, trustful home of early years. I will add, in order to explain one of the similes, that the Arabs believe the huge substructures of Baalbek and Tadmor were brought by the genii, slaves of Solomon.

NOTE 7, *page* 177.

At Hucknall Torkard, the sexton said to me, " You are now standing just over where the head lies."

NOTE 8, *page* 183.

The great composer grew deaf toward the close of his career. And, on one occasion, after conducting one of his own great symphonies, he was touched on the shoulder by another person, in order that he might turn and see the rapturous welcome which he could not hear.

NOTE 9, *page* 192.

The allusion is to the Magdalene, by Correggio, and that by D. G. Rossetti, lately exhibited in the Burlington Club.

NOTE 10, *page* 201.

Published in the *Leeds Mercury*, just before the elections, which gave a majority to the Liberals, in 1880, when Mr. Gladstone had expressed his determination not to take office again.

www.ingramcontent.com/pod-product-compliance
Lightning Source LLC
Chambersburg PA
CBHW031830230426
43669CB00009B/1294